Increasing Students' Learning:
A Faculty Guide to Reducing Stress among Students

by Neal A. Whitman, David C. Spendlove, and Claire H. Clark

ASHE-ERIC Higher Education Report No. 4, 1986

Prepared by

 ® Clearinghouse on Higher Education
The George Washington University

Published by

ASHE

Association for the Study of Higher Education

Jonathan D. Fife,
Series Editor

Cite as
Whitman, Neal A.; Spendlove, David C.; and Clark, Claire H.
*Increasing Students' Learning: A Faculty Guide to Reducing
Stress among Students.* ASHE-ERIC Higher Education Report
No. 4. Washington, D.C.: Association for the Study of Higher
Education, 1986.

Cover design by Michael David Brown, Inc., Rockville, MD.

The ERIC Clearinghouse on Higher Education invites individuals
to submit proposals for writing monographs for the Higher Education Report series. Proposals must include:
1. A detailed manuscript proposal of not more than five pages.
2. A 75-word summary to be used by several review committees
   for the initial screening and rating of each proposal.
3. A vita.
4. A writing sample.

Library of Congress Catalog Card Number 86-82076
ISSN 0884-0040
ISBN 0-913317-31-4

ERIC® **Clearinghouse on Higher Education**
The George Washington University
One Dupont Circle, Suite 630
Washington, D.C. 20036

ASHE **Association for the Study of Higher Education**
One Dupont Circle, Suite 630
Washington, D.C. 20036

*Office of Educational
Research and Improvement
U.S. Department of Education*

This publication was partially prepared with funding from the
Office of Educational Research and Improvement, U.S. Department of Education, under contract no. 400-86-0017. The opinions
expressed in this report do not necessarily reflect the positions or
policies of OERI or the Department.

EXECUTIVE SUMMARY

What Is the Relationship between Teaching and Learning?
The purpose of this report is to help college faculty
increase students' learning by reducing stress among students. Because this report addresses the role of teachers
and students, it is helpful first to explore the relationship
between teaching and learning. The relationship between
teacher and learner essentially poses problems of human
relations. Teachers bring more than knowledge to the relationship; they are motivators, experts, judges. Teachers
and learners share responsibility for learning, and some
question whether "teaching" has occurred if no "learning" occurred.

Studies of teaching that produces the most learning suggest that "effective" teachers use an analytical and syn-
thetic approach to the subject matter, organize the material
well to make it clear, and establish rapport with their students. Most studies identify enthusiasm as important in
promoting students' learning. The key seems to be to make
college courses challenging but not threatening.

How Does Stress Affect Learning?
Many stress models emphasize a "mismatch" between the
individual and his or her environment. Both too little and
too much stress inhibit learning. Stress is difficult to define
because individuals react to it very differently, and a situation that is stressful for one person may not be for another.
Further, stressed individuals vary widely in the effectiveness of their coping.

Some college students, when stressed by academic
demands, use ineffective mechanisms for coping: They
may use "defensive avoidance," for example, avoiding
studying and putting off writing assignments. Teachers can
help such students develop more effective mechanisms for
coping through "stress inoculation"—managing their
courses so that students have information about what to
expect, giving feedback on their progress, and providing a
degree of control over course activities.

What Is the Value of Feedback and Control?
Feedback is information about current performance that
can be used to improve future performance. When given
properly, feedback can encourage positive stress that moti-

vates students to action and can discourage the negative stress that inhibits action.

Teachers can take specific steps to give effective feedback: (1) helping students know where they stand, (2) setting up "learning loops," (3) providing written comments on students' work, (4) testing often enough, and (5) arranging personal meetings to discuss students' work.

Having a personal sense of control is an important factor in reducing stress. When students do not know what to expect in their courses, they feel out of control. Teachers can help students have a greater sense of control by using requests rather than commands, giving students choices in course requirements, explaining assignments so students know their purpose, involving students in the design of examinations, and soliciting and using feedback from students to improve courses and teaching.

College teachers who can effectively use feedback and control in their classroom create a climate ripe for learning. Students are relaxed but motivated to learn when they have an instructor who provides direction and feedback and who is willing to accept it in return.

What Is the Value of Interaction between Faculty and Students?
Studies of college teaching support the view that the frequency and quality of teachers' contact with students, inside and outside the classroom, affect students' involvement in their own learning. Positive teacher-student relations have been linked to students' satisfaction with college, their educational aspirations, and their academic achievement. And when students perceive their teachers as partners in the educational process, they are more likely to take on new and difficult tasks.

To improve their relationships with students and enhance students' learning, teachers can provide structure at the onset of a course, encourage class participation, get to know students by name, mobilize student tutors and study groups, use appropriate humor and personal stories, be "professionally intimate," be accessible outside of class, develop advising skills, and be open to the role of mentor.

In general, students feel less stress and cope more effectively with stress if they feel they belong to the academic community. Faculty can play a key role in introducing and welcoming students to that community.

What Is the Value of Stress Awareness?
While teachers are not therapists, they can be helpful to stressed students. By demonstrating "friendly" attributes, teachers can become aware when students are stressed and help them cope more effectively. Specifically, they might help students with stress reactions, maximize the outcome of meetings with students, recognize severe stress that warrants referral to professional mental health counselors, and disclose their own thoughts and feelings about the course work.

The dropout rate between freshman year and expected graduation year may be as high as 50 percent. For many students, dropping out of school represents a personal loss and failure; for many students in school, ineffective coping contributes to clinical depression. Suicide is a tragic consequence that possibly could be avoided by greater self-awareness. While faculty are not responsible for the well-being of those they teach, college teachers can make an important difference.

What Can Students Do to Increase Their Learning?
Professors should keep in mind that the goal is not to eliminate all stress but to help students develop a variety of skills to cope with the negative aspects of stress.

To assist students, faculty can recommend a number of strategies: (1) improving study habits, (2) managing time wisely, (3) learning positive self-talk, (4) learning how to relax, and (5) joining a student support group.

If students try strategies for coping and still experience the negative aspects of stress, then faculty should encourage students to seek professional counseling or therapy. This suggestion will more likely be received and acted upon if a good relationship between teacher and student already exists and if teachers are aware of what stress is.

Concluding Recommendations
The guiding principle of stress reduction is stress inoculation, suggesting a preventive approach so that the negative aspects of stress can be avoided. Stress inoculation involves giving people realistic warnings, recommenda-

tions, and reassurances. Hence, this report focuses on the value of feedback, faculty-student relationships, and stress awareness.

Stress inoculation is associated with giving people information. Yet little research in the field of higher education describes how best to inform students about the challenges of higher learning. Research in the field of combat and health care shows mixed results regarding the value of information. Thus, a need exists to identify the factors that influence the helpfulness of information in reducing stress.

More research is needed to identify the constructive side of professional intimacy, self-disclosure, and mentoring. Further research could determine why and how teacher-student relationships deteriorate and help faculty construct more successful relationships.

Further research is needed to describe the learning that occurs when one teaches another. Research at lower levels suggests that "to teach is to learn twice." Better understanding this phenomenon at the level of higher education could lead to new teaching strategies. And more research is clearly needed to understand stress among faculty.

ADVISORY BOARD

CONSULTING EDITORS

Richard Alfred
Associate Professor and Chair
Graduate Program in Higher and Adult Continuing Education
University of Michigan

G. Lester Anderson
Professor Emeritus
Pennsylvania State University

Robert C. Andringa
President
Creative Solutions

Robert Barak
Deputy Executive Secretary
Director of Academic Affairs and Research
Iowa State Board of Regents

John B. Bennett
Director
Office on Self-Regulation
American Council on Education

Carole J. Bland
Associate Professor
Department of Family Practice and Community Health
University of Minnesota

Larry Braskamp
Assistant to the Vice Chancellor for Academic Affairs
University of Illinois

Judith A. Clementson-Mohr
Director of Psychological Services
Purdue University

Mark H. Curtis
President Emeritus
Association of American Colleges

Martin Finkelstein
Associate Professor of Higher Education Administration
Seton Hall University

Andrew T. Ford
Provost and Dean of College
Allegheny College

FOREWORD

Many have expressed great concern about maintaining and/
or improving the quality of education at the postsecondary
level, especially student learning. This is not to imply that
a myriad of band-aid solutions have not been applied. For
instance, some have raised admissions standards, believing
that if only top students are admitted, then academic quality can be attained. Another school of thought subscribes to
the Protestant work ethic often known as 'no pain, no
gain,' in which academic quality is assured only through
rigorous, demanding curricula taught by iron-fisted faculty.
If a course does not stressfully challenge students com-
pletely, then it cannot be wholly worthwhile. Conversely,
a course that is enjoyable and stress-free is lacking in
quality.

As doctors, psychologists, and counselors have known
for years and are gradually making the public aware, a certain amount of daily stress is necessary and useful, but too
much stress is dangerous and even abusive. Positive stress
develops a sense of urgency, challenging a person to put
forth his or her best effort at a given task. It enables the
individual to order priorities, heighten concentration, and
buttress desire. Negative stress, on the other hand, tends
to inhibit direction, paralyze action, cripple the learning
capacity, destroy inquisitiveness, and disrupt activities.
The difference between positive and negative stress is one
of control. When students feel that they are in control of
their lives and their time, they remain eager, curious, and
caring. But when they perceive that they are out of control
and can no longer make rational decisions about how they
spend their time, they become withdrawn, inhibited, and
dull. In the movie *Ordinary People,* Conrad, played by
Timothy Hutton, answers his psychiatrist's question of
what is wrong by saying, "I want to feel like I'm in control
of my life, you know." The feeling of control can be a life
or death difference. Considering that in the last decade,
300,000 people between the ages of 15 and 24 killed themselves, it seems obvious that young people are especially
prone to overreacting to stress.

Often faculty set the level of stress to which students are
subjected. By their course workload, personal attitude, and
accessibility, faculty can be a source of positive or negative stress to students. The important role that faculty play
is made clear in this report written by Neal Whitman,

Increasing Students' Learning   xiii

David Spendlove, and Claire Clark, colleagues at the University of Utah School of Medicine, and co-authors of the 1984 report, *Student Stress: Effects and Solutions*. The authors first discuss the impact of stress on learning, then offer precise faculty guidelines for causing, recognizing, and reducing stress. Sometimes a fairly simple change in teaching manner or attitude can make a world of difference to students. Most important, this book teaches professors how to identify stress that is reaching a crisis state.

Although this report is directed to faculty, it is also a valuable reference tool for deans and administrators. Stress is stress, regardless of the origin, manifestations, or recipient. Counselors will undoubtedly recognize many of the symptoms and signs described here. Since colleges and universities by nature gather together many different types of people, making the community as free of negative stress as possible will create a more effective environment.

Jonathan D. Fife
Series Editor
Professor and Director
ERIC Clearinghouse on Higher Education
The George Washington University

WHAT IS THE RELATIONSHIP BETWEEN TEACHING AND LEARNING?

A recent ASHE-ERIC Higher Education Report (Whitman, Spendlove, and Clark 1984) that discussed student stress in higher education identified mostly *institutional* solutions to student stress, including, for example, improving freshman orientation and using student peers as counselors. The focus of this report is the role of faculty, and the purpose is to help college faculty increase students' learning by reducing stress among students.

It is helpful first to explore the relationship between teaching and learning, a complex process:

> *How students learn and how teachers teach are complicated processes, difficult to understand and even harder to master. It is not surprising that professors of many years experience feel they have never quite got it right, and are amazed and gratified when the will to learn and the desire to teach come together in a few moments of excitement, pleasure, and joyful discovery* (Schwartz 1980, p. 235).

What is responsible for those few moments? "The best college courses and teachers so involve students that they learn as much as they can and think about the subject outside the classroom" (Lowman 1984, p. 182). Moreover, "instructors who are excited by their subject . . . foster student enthusiasm by personal example. Teacher enthusiasm infects lectures and discussion and can spread to students' work outside class" (p. 183).

While teachers cannot make students learn, they can promote learning by helping students become motivated to learn, handle information and experience, develop knowledge, attitude, and skills, and transfer their learning from the classroom to the real world (McLagan 1978). In addition to the general role of the teacher as helper, the literature on the relationship between teaching and learning identifies three specific roles: the teacher as *human relations specialist,* as *facilitator,* and as *motivator.* Each role is key to promoting students' learning.

The complexity of the teaching-learning process and its implications for the teacher's role were identified nearly 30 years ago (Bradford 1958). Teachers bring more to the teacher-student relationship than knowledge; they bring an awareness that "the teaching-learning process is basically

The literature on the relationship between teaching and learning identifies three specific roles: the teacher as human relations specialist, as facilitator, and as motivator.

a delicate human transaction requiring skill and sensitivity in human relations'' (p. 136). Furthermore, the relationships between teachers and learners are "precarious because of the anxieties of the learner, the threat of the teacher as a judge and expert, and the mixed feeling held by the learner about his dependency on the teacher'' (p. 136).

The importance of the teacher-learner relationship to students' learning is underscored by 10 guidelines for the teacher as facilitator of student learning:

1. Human beings have a natural potential for learning.
2. Significant learning takes place when the student perceives the subject matter as relevant for his own purposes.
3. Learning involving a change in self-organization—in the perception of oneself—is threatening and tends to be resisted.
4. That learning that is threatening to the self is more easily perceived and assimilated when external threats are at a minimum.
5. When threats to the self are low, experience can be perceived in a differentiated fashion and learning can proceed.
6. Much significant learning is acquired through doing.
7. Learning is facilitated when the student participates responsibly in the learning process.
8. Self-initiated learning involving the whole person of the learner—feelings as well as intellect—is the most lasting and pervasive.
9. Independence, creativity, and self-reliance are all facilitated when self-criticism and self-evaluation are basic and evaluation by others is of secondary importance.
10. The most socially useful learning in the modern world is the learning of the process of learning, a continuing openness to experience and incorporation into oneself of the process of change (Rogers 1969, pp. 157–66).

Students and teachers share responsibility for motivating students (Spitzer 1976, pp. 9–10).

1. *Motivation is the result of the interaction between personal and environmental factors.* Teachers can, for example, create a physical environment that encourages sharing and reduces barriers between teacher and students (McLagan 1978). In small classes, the teacher could arrange the chairs in a semicircle rather than in rows; in a large class, the teacher can move about the room rather than stand behind a podium.
2. *A primary personal factor is that students' feelings influence their thinking.* Teachers can motivate students by showing they understand the student's situation and by respecting learners and their attempts to contribute to the class (McLagan 1978).
3. *Particularly important motives in goal-directed behavior are the need for achievement and the fear of failure.* Thus, teachers help motivate students by giving positive feedback when it is deserved and by giving negative feedback that is not demeaning or belittling.
4. *If the need for achievement exceeds fear of failure, the individual will approach a task; if fear of failure exceeds the need for achievement, the individual will avoid the task.*
5. *Motives can be taught and changed.* No instructor can make students learn, but while teachers are not responsible for differences in ability, they can encourage and expect students to do their best. "College teachers have as much power to dampen students' enthusiasm for learning as excite it" (Lowman 1984, p. 4).
6. *People with a high need for achievement require a standard of excellence by which to evaluate their own performance.* Thus, by providing "feed-forward," teachers can let students know from the start what success looks like. For example, an instructor could make available for students' review term papers that received A's in previous years.
7. *People with a high need for achievement prefer clearly defined goals, and they tend to work hardest when their efforts will make a substantial difference in the final outcome of a project.*

8. *Expecting success is the most powerful single force in human motivation. People with a high need for achievement thrive on moderately uncertain outcomes (probability of success of approximately 0.50); individuals with a high fear of failure thrive on very simple and certain tasks.*

9. *Incentives are important in motivating humans, but extrinsic incentives can overpower the intrinsic satisfaction obtained from successful achievement.* Recognizing that older students are paying a personal price to go back to school, a teacher might keep in mind and mention where appropriate incentives to help learners want to learn—for example, health, time, and money (McLagan 1978).

10. *Most people tend to prefer challenging tasks, especially if the danger of failure is not too great.* Thus, when assigning tasks like making an oral presentation and conducting a research study, teachers should look for cues of frustration and anxiety that signal too much or too little challenge.

11. *The organizational climate can decisively affect motivation.* For example, while letting students know that the teacher is willing to develop course objectives, an instructor could let students know that they are responsible for customizing those objectives to meet their individual needs (McLagan 1978).

12. *Humans tend to gain greatest satisfaction from outcomes that can be attributed to effort, not ability; ability is generally viewed as not being directly under the individual's control.*

13. *Motivation persists and can transfer from task to task until satisfied.* Thus, a well-organized course can increase the likelihood that students will experience the intrinsic satisfaction of knowing they are moving along the right track (Ericksen 1984).

14. *Curiosity, exploration, and the need for competence are fundamental, innate human motives.* Students come to class on the first day wondering what lies ahead. A teacher can help motivate students by letting them know from the start what major issues will be explored and what important questions will be asked (Ericksen 1984).

The college teacher's role as human relations specialist, facilitator, and motivator recognizes that the role of the college teacher goes beyond transmitting information to students. Most college professors who have thought about their goals describe both cognitive and motivational goals for their courses. Typically, they also want to achieve affective goals like increasing students' interest in the area studied so that they will be motivated to continue learning after they leave college (McKeachie 1979).

In defining the relationship between teaching and learning, some question exists as to whether, in the absence of learning, "teaching" describes the professor's behaviors or actions. One can agree or disagree with the statement that "If the learner didn't learn, then the teacher didn't teach!" Those educators who agree believe that, if no learning occurred, then no teaching occurred either (Meeth 1976). According to this view, "teaching" is analogous to "giving," and by definition, when something is given, something has been received. The teacher thus breathes a soul into the clod.

Other educators disagree, believing that teaching is anything an instructor does that intentionally promotes learning, regardless of whether learning actually occurred (Donald and Shore 1977). According to this view, "teaching" is analogous to "offering." When something is offered, it may or may not be received. In this case, the teacher sows seeds that sometimes fall on fertile soil, sometimes on barren soil.

Both views are valuable. On one hand, it is helpful to use students' achievement as a measure of teaching because what students learn is the basic criterion of educational effectiveness (Biddle 1964; O'Hanlon and Mortensen 1977). In fact, when only the process of teaching is used as a measure of teaching, only half the educational process has been evaluated (Mark 1977).

On the other hand, using students' learning as a measure of teaching incurs some problems, especially when students' learning is equated with their performance on examinations.

The measurement of student achievement in a course has been used as the most defensible criterion of effective teaching, but this is where bats fly out of the trunk, because we do not know to what extent examinations reflect what has been taught. . . . Indeed, some may claim that the examination should challenge the student to go beyond what has been taught (Donald 1985, pp. 13–14).

Other problems exist: differences in the difficulty of course objectives, difficulty with measuring some course objectives, the potential abuse by instructors who "teach to the test" (McCarter 1974, p. 32), and the fact that "the best teaching is not that which produces the most learning, since what is learned may be useless" (Scriven 1981, p. 65).

Both views help clarify the relationship between teaching and learning. Teaching and learning make up a two-way process in which the teacher can share, but not assume, responsibility for students' learning. What the teacher does is important, giving the teacher another role—as performer.

Many of you already know what I am about to tell you, but some of you do not. Those who do know—please be patient; there is no need to be bored or insulted. Look on it, please, as a performance. My subject is beautiful, even if it is familiar; I hope I can deliver it in an appropriate style. You do not complain, when you attend a concert, that you have heard Beethoven's Seventh Symphony before, do you? Well, the Law of Cosines is just as lovely a monument to the human spirit (Raimi 1981, p. 59).

The theme of this report is that a teacher's performance is important as it relates to students' learning. "The teacher's performance that prompts witnesses to say he is a good teacher is not always equivalent to good teaching if good teaching is what produces good learning (Machlup 1979, p. 376).

A study of effective teaching that will produce the most learning identifies five components of teaching that distinguish the best from the worst teachers (Hildebrand 1973):

1. *An analytic/synthetic approach.* Good teachers have command of the subject, but this scholarship is not that of the specialist sequestered in the ivory tower. Rather, it is scholarship that couples learning with

adventure. "Does this instructor analyze and show conceptual understanding? Does he contrast the implications of different theories and present the origins of ideas and concepts? Is he a participant in the quest; does he know the other explorers and have a vision of the path ahead?" (p. 46).

2. *Organization/clarity*. Can the teacher get the subject across, not by showmanship and entertainment but by having the facility to make himself clear? That facility is "characterized by the well-chosen example and apt analogy, the progression of ideas and gathering of interest, the placement of emphasis and timely summary" (p. 46).

3. *Instructor/group interaction*. Can the teacher establish rapport with the class, including the ability to control the group's participation and interaction and to know whether students understand the material. A teacher's personality comes through through this component of teaching.

4. *Interaction between instructors and individual students*. Can the teacher establish rapport with individual students? This event can occur in the classroom when the teacher responds to a student as well as in the teacher's office or living room. When a teacher establishes positive interactions with a student, the student is likely to value his counsel, respect him, and want to be like him.

5. *Dynamism/enthusiasm*. "How can one *not* respond to the instructor who is excited about his subject, radiates self-confidence, and loves to teach?" (p. 46). This component of good teaching includes having a varied and distinctive style and a sense of humor.

To help college faculty become better teachers by increasing students' learning, this report reviews and discusses the literature describing the impact of college teachers on stress among students. The major finding is that students learn less when too much *or* too little stress is present. The key is making college courses challenging but not threatening.

HOW DOES STRESS AFFECT LEARNING?

The effects of stress on learning have been studied in animal and human psychology. Experiments with animals conducted at the turn of the century (Yerkes and Dodson 1908) demonstrated that laboratory mice under no stress or extreme stress learned less, while mice under moderate stress learned more. This curvilinear relationship, in the form of an inverted "U" and known as the Yerkes-Dodson law (see figure 1, p. 10), has been used to describe human learning behavior as well (Hockey 1979; Mandler 1982).

Kurt Lewin demonstrated the Yerkes-Dodson law in a study of school children (Bossing and Ruoff 1982). He divided children into three classrooms with teachers who were instructed to be demanding and highly authoritarian in one classroom (a high level of stress), nondirective or laissez-faire in another (low level of stress), and democratic in the third (optimum level of stress). In the authoritarian classroom, students were initially most productive, but over several weeks their resulting aggressive behavior began to reduce the high level of productivity. The laissez-faire teaching style resulted in the lowest levels of productivity and produced levels of aggressive behavior that were almost as high as the first group. The democratic style in which the teacher regularly involved students in discussion about what best to study and how was the best at motivating students, ensuring the highest level of productivity, and reducing group members' frustration.

To implement techniques that will motivate students to the optimum extent—to help them be challenged and not threatened by their learning environment—it is important to understand what stress is and how it affects learning.

What Is Stress?
Hans Selye often is considered the father of stress research, yet he, like many others after him, admits many difficulties are associated with defining the vague concept of stress (Selye 1976). He defines stress as a state manifested by a specific syndrome comprised of all the nonspecifically induced changes within a biologic system. Selye, a physician, used this definition to develop a medical model that accounts for both psychological and biological reactions to stress, describing how the body's biochemical defenses mobilize in response to psychological and biological demands. This mobilization process is referred to as the

---

FIGURE 1
THE YERKES-DODSON LAW

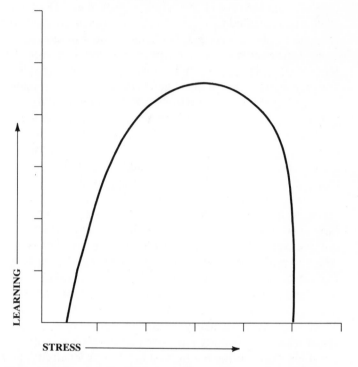

General Adaption Syndrome, a three-stage process that includes an initial alarm reaction to stress followed by a second stage in which the body resists stressors by mobilizing various biochemical resources. If the second stage fails to meet the body's demands, then a third stage occurs that can result in exhaustion and even death. Although Selye's explanation of stress has been used to explain the psychological stress individuals experience, others have shown that the body reacts very differently to stress, depending on whether the stressor is biological or psychological (Baum, Singer, and Baum 1981).

Psychologists and psychiatrists have always had difficulty defining psychological stress in particular, because individual reactions to it are very different. An individual might acknowledge experiencing stress but have any number of reactions to it—anger, fatigue, anxiety, fear, depression, or boredom. Most psychosocial definitions of stress are broad enough to include this wide variety of reactions while focusing on the relationship between the person and the environment. "Stress occurs to the extent that there is some mismatch—actual or perceived—between the person and his or her environment" (Menaghan 1983, p. 158). Another classic study about stress among graduate students defines it as "discomforting responses of persons in particular situations" (Mechanic 1978, p. 7). Yet a third emphasizes "the external and internal forces of stimul[i]" (Lazarus 1966, p. 13). Such definitions do not limit the reactions individuals experience, but they do fall within the context of a person-environment model—probably the most appropriate approach to understanding stress among students.

A situation that is stressful for one person might not be stressful for another. What makes a situation stressful is largely the degree to which it is perceived as such (Lazarus 1966). Consider, for example, two students taking the same college course. One student is threatened by the prospect of not getting an "A" in all classes because it might hurt her chances of being accepted in medical school. She might experience physical and emotional symptoms of stress in the form of high blood pressure and severe anxiety. Another student taking similar courses might feel satisfied with a "B" average—and consequently less stress— because a "B" means being able to attain the college degree necessary to qualify for Air Force flight school training.

What makes a situation stressful is largely the degree to which it is perceived as such.

An important aspect of defining stress illustrated by this example is that what is stressful depends on the *meaning* individuals give to the situation. For the premedical student, A's are critical; even the possibility of not attaining them represents a potential loss in terms of eventually becoming a physician. For the student interested in becoming a pilot, not obtaining an "A" could be merely a minor disappointment. Thus, reactions to the potentially stressful situation can be very different, depending partly on the meaning the situation has for each person.

Stress is also dynamic in that the negative thoughts and feelings associated with stress change depending on one's ✳ ability to cope (Folkman 1982), including the extent to which one continues to define a situation as stressful. The stress level of the premedical student might decrease as she develops interests in other aspects of her life and decides that getting all A's will help her get into medical school but is not necessarily critical. If she is able to believe that getting all A's is not critical, she might be less threatened by potential loss, allowing herself to be more challenged by the material to be learned. In fact, a stressful event that is perceived as challenging is associated with more hope and confidence for the individual, while stress that is perceived as threatening is associated with loss, failure, and avoidance (Lazarus 1966). Thus, the dynamic nature of stress and how it is perceived can allow for the same situation to be viewed differently at different times.

What Are the Effects?
Stress is a very necessary and positive aspect of learning, but it can also be destructive. Research on the effects of stress and thought processes and research on test anxiety identify certain favorable and unfavorable conditions. Stress is most helpful when it requires a vigilant coping pattern from the student (Janis 1982a). A person using vigilance in decision making may search "painstakingly for relevant information, assimilate information in an unbiased manner, and appraise alternatives carefully before making a choice" (Janis 1982a, p. 73). In the process of learning—preparing papers, studying, taking exams—this definition of vigilance is consistent with the hopes many professors have about how students seriously engage in learning.

Stress can also adversely affect learning. When faced with choices, individuals cope with stress in at least four self-defeating ways.

1. *Unconflicted inertia*. Students complacently decide to continue whatever they have been doing, ignoring information about the risk of failure.
2. *Unconflicted change*. Students uncritically adopt the new course of study or learning process that is most salient or most strongly recommended without making contingency plans and without psychologically preparing for setbacks. Such an uncritical approach makes it less likely that a student would think about alternative ways of coping with particularly difficult or unrewarding courses of study and thus be more psychologically vulnerable to such difficulties.

3. *Defensive avoidance*. Students evade studying and other learning activities by procrastinating, constructing wishful rationalizations that support the need not to study, minimizing the negative consequences of not studying, and remaining selectively inattentive to corrective information about the necessity to study.
4. *Hypervigilance*. Students in a paniclike state search frantically for a way out of the stress associated with studies. They rapidly shift back and forth between alternatives to reduce stress and impulsively seize upon hastily contrived solutions that seem to provide immediate relief. Thus, the full range of alternatives is overlooked because of the emotional excitement, repetitive thinking, and cognitive constriction. Students who are hypervigilant are constantly diverted as they try to avoid threatened loss by obsessively and indiscriminately being attentive to information that is both relevant and irrelevant (Janis 1982a).

Alexander Luria, a noted Russian physiologist who explored test anxiety, investigated a paniclike state similar to hypervigilance in the early 1930s (Luria 1932). He classified students as stable or unstable, depending on their behavioral reactions just before taking a test. Those students classified as unstable displayed speech and motor disturbances and became very excited and disorganized before the examination, whereas stable students remained calm. Further independent medical evaluation showed that 61 percent of the unstable students generally manifested "neuropathic symptoms," while only 16 percent of the stable students manifested such symptoms. Luria concluded that examinations evoked emotional reactions so intense that distress before examinations was unmanageable for unstable students.

Another common and generally inadequate way of coping with stress similar to hypervigilance is "attention narrowing" (Mandler 1982), which occurs when one reacts to stress by focusing on one solution. Such an approach can be helpful if the solution happens to be an effective way of dealing with the problem, but one's attention can just as easily focus on irrelevant responses. Individuals who are anxious about a test engage in task-irrelevant behavior that interferes with effective performance on cognitive-intellectual tasks (Spielberger et al. 1978). Such individuals likely display either hypervigilance or attention narrowing, because they are more likely to perceive examinations as more dangerous or more threatening than people with low anxiety about a test and more likely to experience an intense elevation of anxiety in situations in which they are evaluated (Spielberger et al. 1978).

How do anxious students respond when the threat and worry of taking an examination are reduced or eliminated? In a series of small studies (10, 13, and 11 subjects), students were classified into a high test-anxious group and a low test-anxious group (Sarason 1978). Both the high group and the low group were allowed to retake a test they had just taken. The students were told after the first test but before the second test that they could pick the better of the two scores as the final test score. The high group did significantly better on the second test than on the first, while the low group did no better statistically. These results are impressive, given the small sample size, and they appear to support Spielberger's idea that when threat and worry are reduced, test-anxious students become less anxious and thus perform better.

One final reaction to stress that can be reflected by poor performance on an examination is cognitive fatigue. Prolonged exposure to environmental stress, such as extended preparation for a difficult examination, can adversely affect performance (Cohen 1980). Extended preparation can be mentally fatiguing to the point that the student has insufficient reserves to perform well on the examination.

One might question whether the teacher should be responsible for helping students with destructive forms of stress associated with their education. Colleges and universities are after all educationally effective only if they reach students "where they live"—only if they connect significantly with those concerns of central importance to students (Chickering 1969)—and the sources of destructive forms of stress thus become major concerns in the lives of one's students. The research literature offers ways to help reduce severe stress in students and thus help faculty teach more effectively; the following principles can help faculty develop their own methods for reducing stress among students.

People can actually be psychologically "inoculated" against the destructive and demoralizing effects of stress (Meichenbaum 1977, 1985). This notion of inoculation provides a useful framework from which to develop specific programs and techniques to help students. An effective stress inoculation program could be compared to an astronaut's preparation for flight. Before the first liftoff into space, astronauts learn much about what to expect. Numerous simulated liftoffs and space trips prepare them for a wide variety of possible, even predictably threatening, problems. Thus, during the first flight, they are ready for dangerous situations. When students have information about what is expected of them and can predict what will happen (based partly on feedback), they have some idea about how to control problems—even if they never encountered them before—and thus be prepared to cope with stress.

Information, feedback, and control are vital in reducing destructive forms of stress (Seligman 1975) that lead to an intense sense of helplessness and failure. They are necessary for students to learn effectively. Students must have explicit information about what is expected of them and receive relevant feedback about performance so that they can control their learning experience to improve performance.

Another important way to reduce stress focuses on the student-teacher relationship. When students feel that the professor cares not only about their progress in class but also about their academic progress in general and about them as people, they are more likely to feel a collegial relationship with the teacher and adopt the teacher as a role model. In fact, a comprehensive study of stress among law students at the University of Utah found that the support of faculty was even more strongly related to reducing students' stress than the support of their families (Ellinwood, Mayerson, and Paul 1983).

If teachers are to help students with stress, they must be able to recognize it, not only in students but also in themselves. A comprehensive study of stress among university faculty in 80 U.S. institutions (N = 1,920) found that 60 percent of the total stress in the lives of faculty came from their work and that the majority of stressors were related directly to constraints on time and/or resources (Gmelch,

Lovrich, and Wilke 1984). Certainly the stress experienced by the teacher can affect the student and vice versa. Recognizing and understanding students' reactions to stress will help faculty not take personally what is often self-defeating behavior on the part of students.

Finally, increasing one's ability to learn will help students feel more competent and more hopeful about their future as students. Part of what teachers can do is to increase students' abilities to learn by telling them how best to learn from them as teachers. Students can be helped if they know whether they are expected to memorize or to be analytical and, if analytical, exactly what it means and what good examples are.

Faculty can play a key role in creating optimal levels of stress. A carefully documented three-year study of elementary and secondary schools that included over 500 teachers and 10,000 students in experimental and control groups demonstrated that educators could be trained in facilitative skills and that those skills made statistically significant changes in students' attendance, achievement, and self-concept (Aspy and Roebuck 1977). Faculty are encouraged to go beyond the skills identified in this section to create their own plans for optimizing students' stress.

WHAT IS THE VALUE OF FEEDBACK AND CONTROL?

Most college teachers are aware of the importance of feedback and control in the classroom, and they are aware that the way they use feedback and control affects the way students learn. They are also aware that students use feedback and control—though less consciously or systematically—to influence the way teachers teach.

Fewer college teachers are aware, however, that feedback and control also interact with stress to influence learning. Used judiciously, these two techniques encourage the positive stress that motivates students to action and discourage the negative stress that interferes with such action, promoting the moderate level of stress under which students learn most. This section focuses on feedback and control as two techniques to help accomplish that goal.

Feedback

A dominant pattern for teaching and learning is often based on the sequence of test, response, and feedback, where feedback is narrowly interpreted as knowledge of results or outcome. In some cases—memorizing a fixed response, for example—this interpretation is adequate, but in most cases it is a deficient method of evaluating complex learning. Because most college-level learning is complex, this section focuses on more formative than summative feedback, on growth rather than grades (Scriven 1967).

Help students establish their academic status early

Many college students, especially first-year students, endure many weeks or even an entire semester of class-work in a state of uncertainty as to where they stand academically (Nedlands College of Advanced Education 1980). To know rather than wonder where they stand would free those students from the stress of the "status battle" and enable them instead to devote their energies to their courses. Faculty can help by setting up opportunities early in the semester that will provide immediate feedback to students—for example, short assignments, worksheets, or discussion sessions. Teachers can divide large classes into small discussion groups, providing each group with a list of questions to answer or key concepts to learn. In small classes, where verbal exchange is more manageable, teachers can guide discussion through questions, case studies, thought-provoking dilemmas, and so on. Any teaching methodology (having taken class size into consideration) that provides students with immediate or short-term feedback is useful in making students more aware of their academic status. Armed with this information, they can adjust their focus and hours of study time accordingly.

Testing early in the semester is another source of information students can use. If performance on a test is poor, the student still has time to get help or to study more. This sense of control will likely keep stress at a motivating rather than debilitating level.

In addition to early testing, frequent testing is an important factor to consider. Frequent testing fits well with the position that learning is a process where evaluation ought to be more formative than summative. One final examination at the end of the semester is more likely to measure students' memorization or test-taking skills than problem-solving or applied skills. More frequent testing samples learning at different stages, and the feedback at each test can be used in shaping a more polished final product or performance.

Infrequent testing is associated with higher stress because students must demonstrate what they have learned all at once. Students may feel that the situation is like putting all their eggs in one basket and hoping the instructor brings the right basket (that is, asks the questions he had studied). Over 350 psychology, chemistry, law, and medical students who participated in a study on student stress support this notion. They ranked "examinations too infrequently" as more stressful than "examinations too frequently" (Heins, Fahey, and Leiden 1984).

Extreme anxiety associated with testing is also associated with the problematic behavior of cheating. A study of cheating among college students found cheating more highly related to stress than to any other factor (Barnett and Dalton 1981). For the test-anxious student, any type of testing environment provokes anxiety; nevertheless, more chances to demonstrate competence through more frequent testing dramatically reduce the anxiety of a one-shot performance.

Faculty should consider testing at any logical break in subject content and experiment with different ways of testing—presentations, essays, and discussions for a small class, frequent small multiple-choice tests to be corrected in class and used as study guides for the more comprehensive final examination for a large class. For some classes, weekly assignments work well too. Many faculty find tests useful as teaching tools to reemphasize weak areas or points of difficulty.

Use learning loops

Teachers may wonder whether writing comments on a student's paper or even assigning a letter grade will be taken into account in the student's subsequent work. They often complain that students show the same weaknesses again and again and that feedback does not readily transfer from one task to the next (Sadler 1983). Perhaps it is because feedback cannot meaningfully be appreciated unless students are expected to use it—to improve their product. Without this opportunity the following sequence too often results: a student's hard work on an assignment, poor to average appraisal by the teacher, and the class is over. For these students, such an experience is negative. The structure of the class did not allow them to use the teacher's feedback early enough to be able to turn negative events into positive experiences. Thus, an initially motivating stress becomes an interfering stress when access to further learning is cut off, and the stressful situation negatively influences future learning as well for the student who must anticipate subsequent classes taught by the same instructor with the same teaching style.

One solution aimed at short-circuiting escalating stress is to think in terms of a fit between person and environment. Levels of stress are reduced among subjects whose expectations for a given task match the reality of the task (Terence and Sherry 1984). Learning loops—the process of successively shaping students' performances to the desired goal—represent one example of how to work toward such a fit. A similar strategy can be used with examinations. One professor who taught introductory psychology at the University of Utah allowed his students to retake different forms of a test until they achieved the desired grade. Thus, students clearly used feedback from test results to redirect their study efforts and subsequent learning.

Learning loops have long been used for graduate students writing a dissertation. Feedback from an advisor about the initial draft followed by more feedback about the

Levels of stress are reduced among subjects whose expectations for a given task match the reality of the task.

rewritten draft and on and on—and the growing knowledge of excellence along the way—are inseparable and proceed quite naturally. Efforts toward applying this format more routinely for undergraduates will likely result in a consistently higher quality of performance.

Provide written comments, not just grades

Many people consider evaluation and grading synonymous activities. While normative grading is a necessity for certification, accountability, and prediction, grades are "action-neutral" for purposes of improvement. They do little to help students make the connection between their actions and the criteria used to appraise results. Written feedback, on the other hand, makes possible the connection between students' actions and the teacher's appraisal of results. Students given the opportunity to participate actively in the learning process report less stress than those forced into a more passive or helpless mode (Whitman, Spendlove, and Clark 1984).

It is useful to think of feedback as a way of helping students change their behavior, as information about current performance to improve future performance. Feedback to students should be as specific as possible, focused on the important, positive when deserved, and limited to an amount students can use.

Specific. Criticism is more likely to be helpful if it is specific rather than general (Hanson 1975). "This page could be divided into these three paragraphs" is more helpful than "This paper is generally disorganized." Vague comments like "good point" written in the margin do not substitute for sound constructive criticism. The quality of feedback is measured by the extent that it focuses specifically on significant or difficult criteria.

Focused. Typographical errors, sentence construction, paragraphing, and spelling need to be taken into account—but secondarily to the more important issue of content. A stringent test of the meaningfulness of feedback is to ask, "If the weaknesses were corrected, would the work be judged as excellent?"

Teachers in some instances might want to provide their students with a model of good performance. This model, along with their own performance, allows students a means of comparison. Too often feedback or evaluation focuses only on students' performance, and while necessary, it is not always sufficient. To know only *that* one achieved something but not *how* and *why* is only half the achievement. Learning to develop a concept of excellence and the skills and strategies to attain it is the whole achievement.

Positive. Many students come to college with a number of well-developed skills. When they are demonstrated, these skills deserve as much attention for their excellence as do poorly developed skills for their deficiencies. Given attention or positive feedback, desirable behaviors persist; if ignored, however, they tend to be extinguished or to drop out of a repertoire of behaviors (Skinner 1953). In other words, good behavior not only deserves attention but requires it as well.

From the student's perspective, positive feedback from faculty that validates good work reduces the stress of uncertainty because standards of excellence are clarified. Recognition for a job well done increases the likelihood that subsequent jobs will be done well too.

Limited. It is preferable to stretch students' capacity than to bury them. Feedback should be limited to the amount students can use rather than to the amount faculty could give; overloading a person with feedback reduces the probability that it will be useful. When faculty give more feedback than students can use or when it surpasses the level of students' ability, they are more often than not satisfying some need of their own (for example, to control) than trying genuinely to help.

If teachers can follow these points, they will find that these recommendations work against the likelihood of too much and improper feedback.

For all of these points, faculty should be careful that their feedback is understandable (not overly technical or loaded with jargon) and well timed (the more immediate the feedback, the more effective it tends to be). Evaluations of students in the presence of others should be avoided, and feedback should be restricted to constructive criticism of the product not the producer (Hanson 1975).

How might instructors of large classes use these recommendations within a manageable time frame? Many instructors have teaching assistants—often several for very large classes. With minimal training, these assistants can provide excellent written feedback to students. Other instructors, who prefer to make written comments themselves or who do not have teaching assistants, provide written feedback on a predetermined percentage of the total. Thus, every student receives written comments at least once, yet the instructor's time is salvaged. And for some classes it might be appropriate to divide students into small groups and have them critique their peers' papers. With adequate preparation and guidelines, students find this method a very valuable learning experience because of the responsibility they assume in producing a useful critique.

Arrange personal meetings to discuss papers
While personal meetings are not a must for every student or every teacher, they present an opportunity to personalize teaching and to add detail to brief comments on papers. Perhaps more important, they are a rare opportunity for undergraduates to communicate face to face with their instructors. A verbal interchange allows students and teachers several opportunities that would otherwise be lost.

First, students can verify or check feedback. Very often a student's interpretation of a teacher's comments (written or verbal) is not what the teacher intended (Lowman 1984).

Second, students can agree or disagree with the feedback. Students might initially believe their reasoning process was more rational or logical than it really was. The opportunity to exchange ideas with an expert may be what it takes for them to recognize the flaws. On the other hand, some very inquisitive or creative students might introduce novel ideas that justify their disagreement.

Third, humanism in education is encouraged. Personal meetings with students transmit a clear message that they are important and that a student-teacher relationship built on trust and concern is a valuable part of the educational process. Unfortunately, such relationships are probably much more the exception than the rule. While sheer numbers of students (and other faculty responsibilities) preclude teachers' spending too much time with students, it is important not to underestimate the effect they have on students. Several studies examining the student-faculty relationship demonstrate its significant effect on stress and learning. For example, if students see teachers as supportive, this supportiveness is more strongly associated with reducing stress than the support of one's family (Ellinwood, Mayerson, and Paul 1983). In another study, a supportive environment (defined as a college staff that would help first-year students deal with culture shock and assist them in becoming an integral part of the college by providing opportunities for establishing academic status and developing interpersonal skills) was found to be a necessary part of the formula for stress adaptation to take place for first-year college students (Kaplan 1980). And a third study demonstrated that warm and friendly relationships between faculty and students positively affect students' expectations and ambitions (Stevens 1973). Thus, personal meetings with students are not only rewarding, interpersonal pursuits but positively influence academic achievement as well.

Control

I never know what to expect from this teacher! One day he gives a pretty decent lecture and the next day he's off on a tangent. I don't know whether to study what seems to be his personal opinion for the test or stick to the book. And speaking of tests, he refuses to review material with us and is so vague about what will be on them. He never really asks for our opinion on any topic, just dictates his expectations. I wonder if I'm learning anything! The frustrations expressed by this hypothetical student capture the essence of a classroom *without* control. This teacher does not take or give control effectively, leaving students hanging in a state of confusion and anxiety.

Several studies have demonstrated the negative effects that lack of control fosters in students. One, for example, tied students' perceived lack of control (no choices) to greater absenteeism as well as to physical and psychological stress (Rousseau 1976). Two other studies likewise demonstrated that inconsistency creates almost as much stress as rejection (Gibbard, Hartman, and Mann 1973; Martin 1975). Frustrating students' need for predictability is more likely to create significant stress and dissatisfaction than even the absence of a personal relationship with an instructor:

> *Poorly organized or unpredictable classes are especially frustrating. When students are unsure what topics will be covered, what the assignments are, or what the teacher's objectives are, they miss the sense of control that comes from knowing why the challenges that await them were selected and what rules will govern their evaluation* (Lowman 1984, p. 36).

How then can an instructor meet students' needs for mastery and control in the classroom without feeling out of control themselves? The following suggestions are based on Meichenbaum's (1977) stress-inoculation theory that well-used control offers predictability.

Some teachers believe that being liked by students and being firmly in charge are mutually exclusive. They need not be mutually exclusive, however, if the method of control is carefully chosen. Indirect control offers a way to share control between student and teacher that is satisfying to both.

Use requests rather than commands
Selecting words consciously when making assignments encourages suggesting and implying rather than ordering or demanding. For example, the phrases "I would like," "It is my hope," or "You will probably want" should be substituted for "I require" or "You must." Not only will a teacher sound more like a person than an authority; students will perceive that assignments were completed by their choice instead of by the teacher's decree. Using more egalitarian language encourages students' independence and increases the likelihood that assignments will be completed.

Give students choices
Allowing students choices increases their perception of control and reduces their stress dramatically. This suggestion does not include relegating to students the formulation of class objectives or evaluation criteria, but it does include choices about smaller decisions—whether a presentation can be written or oral, whether a paper on a spe-

cific topic could be substituted for an examination. The truly test-anxious student may rightly believe that he can demonstrate a higher level of competence by writing a thoughtful paper than struggling through a test. Choices should, however, be consistent with the instructor's overall course objectives and timetable, and the instructor should not overtly prefer one choice over another.

Justify assignments
Providing a rational justification for assignments is another way to control students indirectly. It can be accomplished in two ways. First, teachers can share their course objectives with students. Understanding the larger picture helps many students see smaller assignments as important means to a desired end, therefore completing them more willingly. Second, if students see the work asked of them as consistent with their own goals, they are less likely to respond to it as busy work imposed by educational authority.

Involve students in examinations
Teachers can involve their students with examinations by preparing them well ahead of time, reviewing them, and asking students to participate in constructing them. Teachers who do so report that they can actually feel classroom tension begin to decrease because students have some control and predictability is increased.

When preparing students for exams, faculty should first check that they are relating test questions to class objectives. A good precaution is to ask, "What did I wish to measure with this question?" Otherwise, many test questions may be peripheral to class content, take students by surprise, and create hostility and stress that will interfere with their testing and learning.

Many instructors are willing to make copies of old examinations for students to use as study guides and concrete examples of what to expect. Doing so forces continual revision of old examinations and updating lectures, a task that results in positive changes for all involved.

For those who teach an introductory course or freshmen, tips on how to answer different kinds of test questions are helpful. It is also helpful to let students know ahead of time the total number of each type of question and which ones require memorization or analysis. This type of preparation offers students predictability and helps them decide how to study efficiently.

Setting aside valuable class time for review may have to be decided for each class. Some students need and appreciate it; others will not attend such a class. Compliant students will attend in any case if a choice is not explicitly given but become frustrated if they have no need for review and increasingly angry that they were not given a choice.

One solution is to let the class decide by a vote. Another is to schedule a review session outside of class hours for students who wish to attend. A third solution when even fewer students are interested is for faculty to invite students with questions to their office or to stay after class. And some faculty feel comfortable allowing students to telephone (even at home) with last-minute questions. This option immediately reduces anxiety for the student who is anticipating problems by allowing him another dimension of control. The actual benefit typically turns out to be psychological (reducing stress) and therefore consumes minimal time for the instructor, because few if any students actually call.

Some instructors make it a practice to develop tests with input from students. For example, the instructor might ask each student to contribute five essay questions *and* answers. Students quickly learn that constructing a good test question is not easy. This method takes as much— usually more—time than studying for a more typical test, yet students almost always react positively to this opportunity. At the very least, they know they will perform well on their own questions, and they appreciate their instructor's confidence in them to share in an important educational task. Typically, students experience a better (more practical) grasp of the material, a greater sense of control, and, in the end, a higher grade. Thereafter, they are much less likely to be as critical of test questions and appreciate them when they are well constructed.

Another related option is to give students take-home tests with a time limit. Many of the same benefits follow, especially those pertaining to increased control and learning.

Solicit and use feedback from students
Students can provide valuable feedback in two ways— directly and indirectly. Directly soliciting feedback uses a

structured format whose purpose is explained and administered during class time. A common example is the course evaluation that all students fill out on the last day of class (Whitman and Weiss 1982). While this standardized feedback has proved very helpful to teachers, it is obviously summative evaluation and so cannot assist with formative decision making. Any undesirable or confusing teaching styles therefore remain undisclosed until the last day, too late for students to feel they had any control. On the other hand, soliciting feedback from students at least once during the semester informs instructors whether class content or teaching techniques need modification *before* they become problems. Some students need little encouragement to volunteer feedback, but unless comments are solicited directly from all students, many valuable and perhaps thoughtful comments will be missed.

One direct method of encouraging feedback is to hand out index cards after two to three weeks of class and ask students to write a comment or question about the instructor personally or about the class content (Lowman 1984). Students need not sign the cards unless they request a reply. This opportunity implies to students that the instructor respects their privacy but also cares about what they think. Paying attention to comments like "You jingle your keys in your pocket and it's distracting" and "Your lectures tend to be dry and boring because you rarely invite classroom discussion" may improve teaching. Most students take seriously the opportunity to critique instructors, appreciating the chance to share some control.

Indirect methods of soliciting feedback from students often work best in conjunction with direct methods. Indirect methods are verbal, unstructured, and unwritten. They depend on the instructor's accessibility, both physical and psychological. To be physically available is to come to class five to 10 minutes early or to stay after class for informal discussion or questions. It also includes posting office hours and being there consistently during those hours. Instructors are psychologically accessible only to the extent that students feel comfortable and welcome approaching them. Intimidated students can rarely or willingly provide feedback. Perhaps even worse, an intimidating or inaccessible instructor creates a generally stressful feeling among students that dampens enthusiasm and interferes with learning.

College teachers who can effectively use feedback and control in their classrooms create a climate ripe for learning. Students are relaxed but motivated to learn because they have an instructor who has provided direction and constructive criticism but also has been willing to accept feedback from students in return.

WHAT IS THE VALUE OF INTERACTION BETWEEN FACULTY AND STUDENTS?

A study designed to assess the development of university students' academic skills (for example, critical thinking, evaluation, and the ability to apply abstract principles) found that students' level of involvement in the classroom was consistently and positively related to reported growth (Terezini, Theophilides, and Lorang 1984). It also found that faculty play an important role through both the frequency and the quality of their contact with students, whether inside or outside the classroom.

Informal faculty-student contact is associated positively with educational outcomes like satisfaction with college, educational aspirations, intellectual and personal development, academic achievement, and continuing after the freshman year (Pascarella 1980). Positive faculty-student interactions are more than "nice to have": They contribute to the educational objectives of higher learning.

How faculty members interact with students has great impact on learning. A number of prominent people (Paul Berg, a Nobel prize winner in chemistry; Beverly Sills, former opera star and now manager of the New York City Opera; Kenneth Clark, noted psychologist and civil rights advocate) who were asked to recall teachers who had influenced them said, "Expectations. Respect. Understanding. Opening windows. These, rather than specific areas, are the characteristics that are repeated over and over" (Hechinger 1980). This chapter suggests specific ways for teachers to interact with students to reduce stress and increase learning.

Provide Structure at the Onset
In many fields—education, science, philosophy, social work, among others—college teachers are urged to go beyond the discovery of new facts and ideas. Instead, learning is defined in terms that go beyond the stage of discovery to those of invention and creation. According to this view, transmitting information to students is neither "unprogressive" nor "unproductive"; rather, it does not go far enough in the educational process. When teachers so enlarge their vision of what is to be taught, they change their roles from "chief purveyors of the truth to that of expert guide in a common search for useful meanings. The class is no longer an audience but a search party, with the teacher at its head" (Schwartz 1980, p. 242).

Positive faculty-student interactions are more than 'nice to have': They contribute to the educational objectives of higher learning.

In this kind of teaching-learning process, students take on tasks that might be new, difficult, often frustrating. Certainty gives way to ambiguity and ambivalence. Learning difficulties are exposed, rather than concealed. Learning moves shakily, in fits and starts, rather than as a gradual accretion of knowledge that fills in the empty spaces of ignorance (Schwartz 1980, p. 243).

What can the teacher do to help students cope with the stress of such learning? They can provide structure at the onset. At the beginning of a course, students need a way of working and a quick beginning into the work itself. During the first session of a second-year social work course, for example, the teacher could define the course and its expectations and begin discussion of the course requirement that each student work with families or small groups in the community, offering to help students find groups and discussing experiences of former students (Schwartz 1980).

Schwartz requires each student to keep a log to enter their comments and observations about the course and their activities. According to one student's log, the opening session provided enough structure to challenge but not threaten the class:

> *Well, things certainly got off to a roaring start—had an incredible class today. I'm about as shook as I expected to be but the shakiness is founded in reality and not just wondering what the class will be like. It's going to be super challenging—he never lets up for a second—push, push, dig, dig, why? why? which is scary but good. Going to have to learn to have enough guts to put myself out and get stomped on* (Schwartz 1980, p. 246).

The need to progress from a relatively high degree of external direction by faculty toward increasing students' self-direction was highlighted in a program of "premeditated evolution" in a required course for freshmen in a business college (Torbert 1978). During the first third of the course, faculty lectured and assigned homework. In the middle third, teaching assistants began to work with students in small groups. And for the last third of the course, students contracted for and carried out self-defined projects, either working alone or in self-selected groups.

These three sequential stages can be generalized to any setting where a teacher or leader "sees some value in encouraging principled work in a community of inquiry, yet doubts whether participants are, at the outset, deeply dedicated to or prepared for active inquiry and principled work" (Torbert 1978, p. 132). Thus, even when independent learning is the desired outcome of a course, teachers provide structure at the beginning.

Encourage Class Participation
Students' levels of involvement in the classroom have been consistently and positively related to reported growth (Terezini, Theophilides, and Lorang 1984). "Whether a class is large or small, successfully handled student participation is an important means by which students assimilate course material and become involved in an atmosphere that supports both personal and academic growth" (Barnes-McConnell 1980, p. 62).

Productive discussions do not just happen, and college faculty may need to develop skills to lead group discussions. An attitude of openness and mutual inquiry is necessary to encourage students' participation and to develop a basic level of trust within students. Developing trust can begin in the opening session by asking students to discuss their personal backgrounds, academic major, and career interests (Barnes-McConnell 1980).

Steps in leading issue-centered discussions include posing an issue, helping students clarify the boundaries of the issue, discussing the issue, and summarizing the discussion (Davis, Fry, and Alexander 1977).[1] Unfortunately, many college teachers are uncomfortable with class participation, perhaps because they have to give up some control over activity in the classroom. When communication is not all one way, students share leadership of the teaching-learning process as well as responsibility for its success or failure. For some teachers, this notion may be a radical one. Certainly, according to one study, professors do the most talk-

1. Teachers who want to develop the skills necessary to lead structured, problem-solving, and issue-centered discussions would do well to consult *The Discussion Method* (Davis, Fry, and Alexander 1977), *A Handbook for Group Discussion Leaders: Alternatives to Lecturing Medical Students to Death* (Whitman and Schwenk 1983), and *Learning in Groups* (Bouton and Garth 1983).

ing, typically 80 percent of the time, even when the class is not a large lecture class (Ellner and Barnes 1983).

One technique to encourage class participation, even in large lecture classes, that will allow teachers to maintain whatever level of control they are comfortable with is to ask students questions and to welcome their questions. When students answer questions, it is important not to belittle them when they are wrong. And the request for questions must be sincere, not like the chairman of the board in a cartoon who snapped, ''Damn it, Crenshaw. When I asked for questions, I was merely using a figure of speech!'' Students' participation in class is key to promoting independent thinking and motivation. Although requiring ''considerable instructor spontaneity, creativity, and tolerance for the unknown'' (Lowman 1984, p. 119), it is the means by which students become personally involved in their own education.

Get to Know Students by Name

Learning students' names is important because it promotes rapport and begins the personal contact that students tend to value highly. One suggestion for alleviating the difficulty of remembering the names of people just met, perhaps resulting from one's own stress, is to get written work from students that can be discussed with them (Eble 1979). Another strategy is to ask students on the first day of class to write their names on index cards and to add anything about themselves they would like the professor to know. After collecting the cards, read off each student's name and match the index card to the face. After every three or four names, review those names. Try to use as many names as possible in the first class session (Lowman 1984).

Whatever the system used, the teacher should let students know he is trying to learn their names. They will likely appreciate the effort and be more patient if the teacher makes mistakes.

Mobilize Tutors and Groups

A major educational principle is *to teach is to learn twice* (Raimi 1981). In fact, faculty often learn more than students when they prepare and present instructional material. Thus, it makes sense that students will learn more when they are placed in the role of teaching each other. In one experiment, two groups of college freshman volunteers recruited from the introductory psychology course were given an article on the brain's functioning. The control group was told that they would be given an examination on the article. The experimental group was told that they would be asked to teach the material to another student. Both groups were asked to spend about three hours studying the article.

Both groups were given the same exam, with each question designed to test either rote memory or conceptual understanding. For the experimental group, the exam was unexpected. Both groups performed equally on the rote memory items, but the experimental group scored significantly higher on the conceptual understanding items. Thus, the process of learning when one learns material to teach it may be different (Benware and Deci 1984). (See also Luepker, Johnson, and Murray 1983; Martin and Newman 1973; Rizzolo 1982; and Telch, Kellen, and McCoby 1982.) If this is the case, some of the positive effects of tutoring could be achieved even before the tutoring occurs. And benefits might also occur during the process of tutoring others, as material is presented and reinforced.

Thus, college teachers should organize student tutorials and study groups. By teaching each other, students can feel more competent and feel more confident that they can master material.

Use Humor and Personal Stories
College teachers often ask whether they should tell jokes in class. Bad jokes are no funnier in the classroom than anywhere else; in fact, they can "create embarrassment, unease, and hostility" (Eble 1979, p. 37). A study conducted at the University of New Mexico confirmed that caution, finding that a teacher's use of humor is "likely to be perceived with suspicion and hostility" (Jacobson 1984, p. 25). According to the researchers at New Mexico, when teachers tell jokes, they contradict students' expectations and make the students feel defensive—whether the humor is derogatory or ridiculing or innocent and void of hostility.

In general, then, teachers should not tell jokes. When humor is not forced and is part of the natural discourse of a class, however, it can be an excellent way to establish rapport with a class (Eble 1979). And faculty should consider using personal stories to lend an air of intimacy to their classes (Barnes-McConnell 1980). A personal story or an anecdote can make teachers more human in the eyes of their students—especially when the story or anecdote shows that even college professors stumble along the path to higher learning. In this regard, one college professor has emphasized the importance of failure in the success process, suggesting that when teachers relive their past difficulties, students can feel relief. Thus, the personal anecdote becomes a means of supporting students' motivation and growth (Barnes-McConnell 1980).

A teacher can use five criteria when judging anecdotes for use in the classroom:

1. Does the anecdote illustrate an important principle?
2. Is listening to it enjoyable?
3. Is the anecdote personal, telling the students something about the teacher as a person?
4. Can students relate to the situation described?
5. Is the anecdote funny? (Mouw 1981).

A general rule of thumb for humor, personal stories, and anecdotes is to be oneself. Students learn best when they feel comfortable, and it will probably occur only when faculty feel comfortable as well.

Be Professionally Intimate

Students' performance is enhanced when teachers are emotionally close to students without necessarily being a personal friend—a delicately balanced relationship termed "professional intimacy" (Whitman and Schwenk 1983). An analogous relationship exists between physician and patient. On one hand, it is neither possible nor desirable for a doctor to make every patient a close, personal friend, and doctors generally do not date patients. On the other hand, it is helpful for a doctor not to hide behind a facade when relating to a patient. Likewise, college teachers should relate to students honestly and openly as a trusted teacher.

Being professionally intimate begins in the classroom. Teachers should consider sharing their thoughts and values in a manner that encourages students to disclose theirs. Teachers can accept diverse opinions without implying that they agree with all opinions. The key to students' development lies in A. Bronson Alcott's dictum stated over a century ago: "A true teacher defends his pupils against his own personal experience." In other words, teachers should reveal—but not impose—their views.

College teachers can further establish professional intimacy in the classroom by being comfortable with students of different abilities and backgrounds. It is particularly important that teachers become committed to the process of personal growth for all students, even for those unlike himself or herself. Students sense when faculty are uncomfortable with or uncommitted to certain types of students, and their motivation may wane.

Professional intimacy also occurs outside the classroom; when teachers share their interests in campus activities, they may find frequent opportunities to engage students. By being themselves and encouraging students to be themselves, teachers can nurture meaningful and appropriate relationships.

Faculty who are professionally intimate often become role models for students. One cannot *tell* someone else how to be but can *show* them and by example make being that way seem desirable and worthwhile.

Be Accessible Outside of Class
A survey of faculty and students at nine colleges and universities found:

> *The single biggest difference between influential faculty and their colleagues is the extent to which they interact with students outside the classroom....[The] evidence indicates that a college teacher's chances of being regarded as effective are significantly affected by the extent to which he interacts with the students beyond the classroom* (Gaff 1973, p. 609).

Additional studies have supported similar conclusions. One study of large private universities in the Northeast concluded that student-faculty informal relationships may significantly influence students' academic performance (Pascarella, Terezini, and Hibel 1978), and another study of a large public university in the Northeast found that faculty play an important role through both the frequency and

the quality of their contact with students (Terezini, Theophilides, and Lorang 1984).

Faculty might take for granted the influence they have
on students outside the classroom. Yet students benefit
from relationships with their teachers in a number of ways.
In one survey, the most common way was just being
"available and open to any discussion" (Gaff 1973, p. 617),
but teachers also provide intellectual stimulation and help
students feel confident in their own abilities. Besides generally motivating students, faculty-student interactions can
help students cope with their stresses. Because college
teachers probably faced similar problems when they were
students, faculty can be empathetic and encouraging.

Most people cope more effectively with their stresses
when they feel that they belong to a community. By establishing relationships with students outside the classroom,
teachers can help students feel that they are members of
the academic community. Students' learning is significantly
enhanced by contact with faculty—in faculty offices and
class building corridors, on the lawns and paths of the campus, even at students' dorms and faculty homes.

Develop Advising Skills
Good advising is a key to improving students' performance. Good advising programs result in better attitudes,
self-concept, intellectual and interpersonal development,
and academic performance, and in increased retention
(Grites 1980). "If academic advising does nothing else, it at
least should provide information [that] helps students make
the decisions to pursue their college careers successfully"
(p. 3). Some may argue that professors are incapable of
keeping details straight and that petty details are beneath
their dignity, but that willingness to provide information is
a matter of will: "It is odd that an institution would trust
professors to master details of vast and complex subject
matters and not trust them to convey accurate information
about requirements for a major" (Eble 1979, p. 75). Thus,
college faculty should develop an ability to correctly advise
students regarding academic requirements. Moreover, a
helpful answer to a student's question might be the first
step in a more meaningful exchange about other important
matters.

Good advising also requires good listening. The important emotional messages that may be present when a student sees a teacher need to be heard. Sometimes these messages are hidden, and faculty have to listen carefully. Other times they are overt, and students simply need to feel that someone has heard them. One helpful listening skill is for teachers to paraphrase what students have asked or said. Although it may take a special effort to make student advising more than a token relationship, "this effort might be the significant factor in the student's academic success or failure, satisfaction or discontent, and retention or attrition" (Grites 1980, p. 4).

Be Open to the Mentor's Role
The ultimate faculty-student interaction occurs between a mentor and his or her disciple. Not all teachers become a mentor, and not all students have one, but those who have had a mentor may experience long-lasting effects.

The mentor—someone who, as a role model, shows others how to be and, by example, makes being that way seem desirable and worthwhile—has several functions:

He may act as a teacher to enhance the young man's skills and intellectual development. Serving as sponsor, he may use his influence to facilitate the young man's entry and advancement. He may be a host and guide, welcoming the initiate into a new occupational and social world and acquainting him with its values, customs, resources, and cast of characters. Through his own virtues, achievements, and way of living, the mentor may be an exemplar that the protege can admire and seek to emulate. He may provide counsel and moral support in time of stress. The mentor has another function...developmentally the most crucial one: to support and facilitate the realization of the Dream (Levinson 1978, p. 98).

The use of the male gender to explain the mentor relationship underscores the almost exclusively male domain of mentoring; women have fewer mentors, male or female, than men. "One of the great problems of women is that female mentors are scarce. . . .The few women who might serve as mentors are often too beset by the stresses of survival in a work world dominated by men to provide good mentoring for younger women'' (Levinson 1978, p. 98).

Mentors play a key role as models, which is how faculty teach attitudes (Whitman and Schwenk 1984). They do so by being capable (demonstrating competence and excellence in teaching and in a chosen field of study), by being enthusiastic (demonstrating energy in their approaches to learning and being themselves continuous learners), and by being themselves (being honest and open with students and thus encouraging students to be self-revealing and self-disclosing).

Teachers who have been a role model for a class of students may find that one student, in particular, will look for something more. Teachers are encouraged to be open to that special role. In addition to providing the student with perhaps his or her most important college learning experience, faculty will grow as a result of the relationship.

Some faculty may be concerned that, given institutional realities, mentoring is not possible because of limited time. If faculty themselves feel stressed by the ''publish or perish'' dictum, then they might avoid the mentor's role. In some cases, however, mentoring can lead to higher productivity in faculty research, including joint investigation by teachers and students.

Conclusion

One criticism of faculty-student relationships is common:

> ...faculty members and students no longer seem to be connecting. Our students do not seem to be involved in learning, they say. We seem to have lost the ability to create a shared community of values; we have substituted diversity for coherence and cannot find our way back to integrating principles (Robin 1985, p. 56).

The reports all seem to ''ignore a very real wish among students and faculty . . . to find a place of meeting'' (p. 56).

A study that asked faculty and students what they worried about most on the first day of class found that the three most common concerns of faculty were ''Will the students get involved?'' ''Will they like me?'' and ''Will the class work well as a class?'' Students' three most common were "Will I be able to do the work?" "Will I like the professor?" and "Will I get along with my classmates?"

[Although] there was a real desire on the part of both students and faculty for connectedness,. . .neither group realized that the other shared that desire. If participants on both sides don't understand how to develop their relationship, learning will be diminished (Robin 1985, p. 56).

Thus, faculty-student interactions are valuable. Positive relationships with faculty, inside and outside the classroom, can help reduce students' stress and help them cope more effectively with stress. Faculty can play a key role in introducing and welcoming students to the academic community, beginning with the classroom as a microcosm of that community and extending outside the classroom as well.

WHAT IS THE VALUE OF STRESS AWARENESS?

While teachers are not therapists, effective teachers can be good friends to their students (Ericksen 1984)—can be professionally intimate. The characteristics of friendship are understanding, trust, respect, confidence, mutual assistance, enjoyment, acceptance, and spontaneity (Davis 1985). A teacher who demonstrates friendly attributes may be in a position to recognize the stress a student is experiencing and, as a friend, help. Thus, a teacher does not have to be a therapist to help students cope with stress.

Helping Students with Stress Reactions
Although the signs and symptoms of stress vary depending on the individual, anxiety, fear, depression, boredom, hostility, dependence, and helplessness are all stress-related signs and symptoms. The causes of stress are usually as different as the various signs and symptoms that the professor observes or the student complains about. One of the most important aspects of stress is that "it is determined by the perception of the stressful situation rather than by the situation itself" (Mikhail 1985, p. 35); therefore, it is important if the professor is to understand what is causing the student's stress that the student's perceptions be explored. The professor could state, "Help me understand what you are so upset about," or "What does it mean to you if you don't do as well on the test as you'd like to do?"

Faculty might respond with anger, frustration, even rejection to students' stress reactions of anger and frustration. If students are to increase their learning ability, however, the faculty member must avoid taking students' stress reactions personally and instead help those students experiencing overwhelming stress recognize their stress and identify the causes by exploring perceptions.

One fairly common stress reaction is to become an anxious-dependent student—one who constantly asks for clarification and black-and-white distinctions and wants to know only what the teacher thinks is important (Lowman 1984). In fact, "the tendency to think in absolute black or white all-or-nothing terms" (Sacco and Beck 1985, p. 5) could reflect a depressogenic cognitive pattern. The negative feelings and behaviors of teachers toward such students will only aggravate students' stress—perhaps in the form of depression.

One fairly common stress reaction is to become an anxious-dependent student—one who constantly asks for clarification and black-and-white distinctions.

Merely telling students to figure out a problem for themselves or suggesting in a punitive way that their questions are inappropriate increases the distance from the teacher without actually changing students' attitudes, behaviors, or stressful feelings. A more useful response to the student's request for a black or white answer might be, *You have brought up a critical issue about learning. It is important that you look at this problem as not necessarily something that has a right answer; you should rather consider the consequences of various actions to deal with the problem. In fact, when you take the test on the subject, I'm not particularly interested in your answer as much as in how you analyze the problem.*

Effective teachers who see their role as a friend of the student will be better prepared to help students who display anxious-dependent behavior. In fact, a thoughtful discussion with the student about how to learn best from the teacher will be more effective in increasing learning than a rude comment that is not intended to teach but to ventilate frustration.

Discouraged or failing students are by definition plagued with stress because of the helplessness often associated with failure. Teachers can play a crucial role in inspiring discouraged students by merely showing enough concern to meet with them and understand their problems (Lowman 1984). Along with showing concern, the teacher can be a resource to failing students by helping them seek appropriate aid—tutoring, counseling, prerequisite courses, study groups, and so on. The teacher who writes or makes positive comments about the student's work is a special help to discouraged students. Positive comments might not seem justified for failing students, yet discovering and recognizing even small improvements can inspire and enhance learning for them.

Many distressed students also display depressive cognitive patterns in the form of self-blame (Metalsky et al. 1982). In a prospective study of 277 undergraduates, Metalsky and his colleagues were able to predict, based on cognitive style, who among students doing poorly on examinations were most likely to display a depressed mood. They found a significant relationship between internal and global thinking patterns and an increased risk for depressive mood after doing poorly on a midterm examination. Students who used an internal thinking pattern tended to personalize their failures highly. The student with an internal style might say to him or herself, "I'm the only one to ever do so poorly on this midterm," while a more external explanation for failure might be, "This test was especially difficult." Internal explanations for failure particularly affect loss of self-esteem after bad events (Peterson and Seligman 1985).

The student who was more likely to be depressed after a poor performance on the midterm was the student who likely attributed poor performance to "the fact that I'm stupid"—a more "global" response. A more "specific" statement would be, "I'm stupid in the subject," and an even more specific comment would be, "I performed stupidly on *this* test." The emotional problems that global thinking creates relate to individuals' generalizing a specific problem to other areas of their life. Global-thinking students might generalize a "D" on a test to such an extent that they begin to see themselves as "D" persons.

Teachers can assist such students by helping them see their failures in less internal, more external terms—by saying, for example, "Most students occasionally do poorly on tests, but you'll have many other opportunities to see that you can manage your studies." Teachers can also help students who see themselves as generally stupid (engaging in global thinking) by helping them specify their "stupid" behavior. A professor might say to such a student, who is confused about his course work, "John, you seem to be upset. You're having a difficult time understanding this concept, and as a result you question whether you should even be taking this class. But you've been doing fairly well to this point, and from what you've said, this is the first problem you've had with the course. Let's hang in there a little longer."

Besides thinking in black-and-white or all-or-nothing terms, depressed individuals tend to magnify the significance of undesirable events and minimize the significance of desirable events (Beck 1967), tending to draw negative conclusions about events in the absence of evidence. The depressed student might "know," for example, that the teacher thinks he or she is stupid when actually no evidence suggests that the teacher thinks that way—and in fact the evidence might be to the contrary. Individuals who are experiencing major depression exhibit other thinking and feeling states: feelings of worthlessness, self-reproach, excessive or inappropriate guilt (American Psychiatric Association 1980), indecisiveness, complaints about diminished ability to think, and suicidal thoughts.

Meeting with Students

The student under stress who arranges a formal meeting with the professor or drops by during office hours is not doing so casually. The decision to see the teacher has likely been considered and carefully thought out, and it is therefore important to treat the student in an especially respectful manner. The anxiety and fear or discomfort that the student carries into an interview with a teacher is probably not much different from those feelings the teacher might carry into a visit with the dean of the college. The teacher can help most by being or (if necessary) acting eager and interested to talk with the student. Being late or not being available during office hours only increases the student's sense of helplessness, frustration, and anger.

When the student wants to discuss an issue that will obviously take more time than scheduled, it is important to plan another meeting rather than to hurry the student. The teacher should avoid giving nonverbal cues (looking at the clock, looking uninterested, opening mail) that indicate he is in a hurry. It is better to be direct about the limited time so that students will understand rather than indirect, in which case students are likely to interpret the behavior as rejection and lack of interest. A good way to let students know that his or her concerns are important is to have the secretary take a message when the phone rings.

It is easy for the teacher to mistakenly assume he knows what the student is most concerned about. It is often helpful to focus on the student's greatest concern by asking, "John, of all the things you have discussed, what are you most concerned about?"

It is important not to quickly offer a solution. Quick and simple answers will likely leave the student feeling confused instead of feeling carefully understood. Even when a solution seems obvious to the teacher, it is important to hear the student out, then help him or her form solutions, being cautious about the advice offered.

when in fact many other students are having difficulties. This sense of "only-ness" leaves them feeling depressed because they attribute their difficulties almost exclusively to inadequacies within themselves rather than appreciate that their fellow students might also have to struggle to understand concepts. Finally, depressed people often think their problems are chronic or never changing. Depressed students who are struggling with their course work might believe they will "always be stupid." Thinking in global, personal, and chronic terms puts individuals at greater risk for depression (see, for example, Peterson and Seligman 1985 for an indepth review of the literature on learned helplessness and depression).

The physical symptoms of major depression include sleep disturbances, significant weight changes, psychomotor agitation, and fatigue or loss of energy (American Psychiatric Association 1980). Depressed patients often find themselves waking during the night and having difficulty falling back to sleep. Some people might gain excessive amounts of weight; others lose their appetites and experience weight loss.

Depressed individuals describe themselves as feeling sad, blue, guilty, and disappointed in themselves. In fact, they usually "look" depressed. (Some individuals, however, can maintain a "happy" facial expression even though they are deeply depressed.) Not only do depressed individuals usually look depressed; they often behave in a depressed manner. They cry more than usual, they spend less time with friends and relatives, and they act more irritated than they did before they were depressed.

Moderately to severely depressed people commonly have suicidal thoughts. A person who can demonstrate caring and concern needs to listen carefully to such thoughts. Keeping someone from expressing his suicidal thoughts is not helpful, and most people find it a relief to tell someone about such thoughts. Usually suicidal thoughts are expressed indirectly; the student might say, "I'm not sure it's all worth it" or "I don't think I'll be around next semester anyway." It is important to ask the student what he or she means by such a statement. Asking the student to clarify it shows not only that the teacher is interested but also that it is acceptable for the student to express more serious thoughts and feelings. During such conversations, it is important to recommend unequivocally to students that they seek professional help and that they not hurt themselves. It is also important that the teacher let such students know that he appreciates their trust and would like to see them again, especially after they have found professional help. It is not necessary or appropriate to be the student's therapist, but concern and contact can be very helpful.

Some people are obviously more at risk for suicide than others and need professional help immediately. Students with a definite plan about how and when they will kill themselves are more at risk than those without such a plan. Those who plan more violent means of killing themselves—using a gun or jumping from a building—are typically more at risk than those who plan to take pills. Those who express a profound sense of hopelessness about their future are more at risk than those who talk about the future and what they will be doing. Those who have admitted preparing for suicide by writing a will or giving away their possessions are more at risk than those who have not made such arrangements (see, for example, Boyer and Guthrie 1985; Comstock 1984; and Litman and Farberow 1961 for more information on the potential for suicide).

The vast majority of people who have killed themselves gave clues before their death about their wanting help. Asking a student what he means when he said it was not worth it might actually prevent a suicide or an attempted suicide.

Self-disclosure and Self-awareness

Every maladjusted person is a person who has not made himself known to another human being and in consequence does not know himself. Nor can he be himself. More than that, he struggles actively to avoid becoming known. A person provides for himself a cancerous kind of stress [that] is subtle and unrecognized but nonetheless effective in producing not only the assorted patterns of unhealthy personality . . . but also the wide array of physical ills that have come to be recognized as the province of psychosomatic illness (Jourard 1971, p. 32).

Self-awareness and self-disclosure are important. Disclosing to students one's own thoughts and feelings as they relate at least to the course work not only helps improve the relationship with students but also helps one identify and become aware of important issues in his own work. Being able to recognize and then disclose distress about issues that present themselves in class helps decrease the emotional distance that students and teachers feel toward each other, thus helping reduce stress in the classroom. A teacher who finds himself mildly distressed about comments from medical students regarding the treatment of a particular patient might nonjudgmentally disclose his thoughts and feelings to the students, hoping to lead to a fruitful discussion about attitudes and feelings concerning patient care. As a result, students might become more willing to talk about issues of critical importance to them. Reducing the emotional distance in a student-teacher relationship goes a long way toward reducing students' distress, because they see the teacher as a friend.

The importance of self-disclosure has been well established in psychotherapy (Hansen, Stevic, and Warner 1977) and has been generalized to many other helping relationships, including teaching (Jourard 1971). Numerous studies of clients and therapists show that the level of the therapist's self-disclosure is as important in helping the client as the level of the client's self-disclosure (Hansen, Stevic, and Warner 1977). The therapist's self-disclosing behavior provides a model for the client and enhances the communication between the two; further, it has a positive effect on the client's attendance at sessions and participation in therapy (Giannandrea and Murphy 1973). Clients' self-disclosure has proven desirable because it relates positively to personal adjustment and to successful therapy.

A distinction should be made between self-disclosing behavior on the part of counselors and self-involvement (McCarthy and Betz 1978). Although the distinction reflects merely differences between two types of self-disclosure, these differences are important to consider when helping students. Self-disclosure is "a statement of factual information on the part of the helper about himself or herself" (p. 251), while self-involvement is "a statement of the helper's personal response to statements made by the helpee" (p. 251). Clients rate self-involving therapists as significantly more expert and trustworthy than therapists who use self-disclosing statements. Professors might also offer personal reactions to statements students make and avoid making factual statements about themselves. A self-disclosing statement (as defined by McCarthy and Betz) might be, "When I was a student like you, I often found my course work difficult and frustrating," but a more self-involving statement might be, "It's painful for me to see how confused and frustrated you are about the course I'm teaching." Self-involving statements require a greater degree of personal risk than do self-disclosing statements; such risk on the part of the therapist helps build trust. Furthermore, self-involving statements help keep the focus of the conversation on the client, while self-disclosing statements tend to shift the focus to the therapist (McCarthy and Betz 1978).

The relationship between the therapist's self-disclosure and a positive outcome for the client, however, is not linear (Jourard 1971), for "there is an optimum level of self-disclosure beyond which point it may be destructive either in terms of [an] individual's feelings or in a personal relationship" (Hansen, Stevic, and Warner 1977, p. 259).

The teacher should observe the effects of self-disclosure in the classroom; if students as a result participate more, thus becoming more involved in their own learning, it is having a positive impact. On the other hand, if students do not become more open and in fact seem more distant, then the teacher's self-disclosure should perhaps be discontinued.

One should also experience a certain amount of self-awareness in relationship to stress. The finding that most of the stress in the lives of university faculty can be accounted for by the work environment (Gmelch, Lovrich, and Wilke 1984) is not particularly surprising when one realizes that those in professional occupations who interact with others are more vulnerable to stress than those who work in product-oriented institutions (Cooper and Marshall 1976). The problem is not so much that stress is highly prevalent among faculty in higher education but that when it becomes overwhelming, it adversely affects the professional's productivity, performance, job satisfaction, and health (Buck 1972; Burke 1971).

> . . . teachers with greater stress have more somatic symptoms, higher levels of anxiety, and psychological

difficulties. It . . . is not only clear that job stress nega-
tively affects teachers, which likely affects absenteeism,
health care costs, work fitness, and productivity, but job
stress also affects the classroom environment, the teach-
ing/learning process, and the attainment of educational
goals and objectives (Bossing and Ruoff 1982, p. 27).

Teachers must recognize symptoms of stress in their
own lives so that they can correct the symptoms before
their stress is so destructive that it adversely affects their
productivity and their students' learning. In addition to the
psychological symptoms of stress previously described—
anger, depression, anxiety—loss of sexual interest, excessive smoking, and difficulty sleeping are psychological
signs. But there are physical signs as well—high blood
pressure, increased heart rate—and symptoms—stomach
pain, headaches, backaches, sore muscles, and diarrhea.
Many of the symptoms of stress that teachers likely experience are described in the literature on burnout, which "is
mostly indistinguishable from depression except that it sur-
rounds work [and] in many ways . . . is a 40-hour-a-week
depression" (Peterson and Seligman 1985, p. 931).

Burnout is a syndrome of emotional exhaustion, deperson-
alization, and reduced personal accomplishment. It is a
response to the chronic emotional strain of dealing exten-
sively with other human beings (Maslach 1982, p. 3).

The individual who is emotionally exhausted feels drained
and used up and lacks the energy to face another day.
Emotional exhaustion is at the heart of burnout and occurs in people who get overly involved emotionally, over-
extend themselves, and feel overwhelmed by the demands
of others.

Depersonalization occurs when an individual develops
an increasingly poor opinion of other people, including
expecting the worst of and disliking others. Faculty who
are overloaded with course work and/or supervising graduate students might begin to resent students because they
feel trapped by an inordinate number of demands and high
expectations.

Finally, people begin to feel a lack of personal accomplishment. As they feel guilty about their negative feelings toward others, they also begin to feel a sense of inadequacy in their professional role. Such a view of oneself can be an attack on one's self-esteem and thus lead to depression.

Most of the actions to correct burnout suggested in the literature focus on social and organizational changes and improved interpersonal skills—setting limits on one's work, enhancing time off work, seeking support from others, using humor, exercising, and eating properly (see, for example, Maslach 1982; Paine 1982; and Pines, Aronson, and Kafry 1980).

Self-disclosure and self-awareness are critical in helping faculty enjoy their work and be more effective as caring teachers. It is likely that the effect of burnoutamong faculty is costly, at least in terms of students' learning.

Conclusion
Certainly professors will be in a better position to help students under stress if the university environment is structured to help students. Improved orientation sessions, adequate student' counseling centers, student buddy systems, students' participation in designing curriculum and other programs (Whitman, Spendlove, and Clark 1984)—all create an atmosphere suggesting that it is important and expected that one be aware of and help students with their stress. Such programs might also sensitize and help faculty members.

In addition to these recommendations, however, formal courses might be offered to help both students and faculty learn how to control stress. Such a program has been successful at the University of Maryland (Allen 1981), helping students become more aware of their stress through various measures of self-assessment and methods to look at one's predisposing factors for stress. The courses also teach various stress management skills, including cognitive reappraisal, relaxation exercises, biofeedback training, and social engineering strategies. Participating subjects improved significantly on a number of stress factors when compared to control subjects. Such courses could be particularly helpful to students who otherwise might refuse to go to a student counseling center.

WHAT CAN STUDENTS DO TO INCREASE THEIR LEARNING?

Picture the following scenario. A freshman student comes to your office following a rather dismal performance on the first examination. He has been attending class but participates infrequently. As you talk with him, you note a disheveled appearance, lack of eye contact, nervous hands, and a general air of discouragement. Then he asks, "You know, I'm not doing as well as I think I could be doing or as I've done in the past. I thought maybe you could make some suggestions that would help me get out of this rut I'm sinking into."

First, the goal is not to **eliminate** *stress but to* **moderate** *it.*

As a professor of history or English, your first thought might be that you wish this harried student were making this request of his psychology professor instead. But a second thought quickly emerges: If only I had access, some basic strategies or skills must be available that I could suggest to students-in-need, suggestions that would moderate these typical stresses that can get so out of control.

Many strategies are indeed available for coping that can be very useful in moderating stress. The problem is how to find them without reading a dozen books on the subject or trying to transform theoretical concepts into practical behaviors.

This chapter addresses those needs of accessibility and practicality by providing a number of carefully selected and well-defined strategies for coping. They were selected as strategies a teacher could recommend to a student but whose implementation would be the student's responsibility. The specific strategy or strategies recommended depend on both the needs of the situation and the teacher's judgment of what the student might successfully manage.

Two factors must be kept in mind: First, the goal is not to *eliminate* stress but to *moderate* it. Some stress is motivating. It makes students just anxious enough to study for tests and prepare assignments, thereby challenging them to reach their potential. This "good stress" correlates with maximum learning, while no stress or extreme stress correlates with little or no learning.

Second the goal is to develop a variety of coping skills. Lower stress and higher performance are associated with a broad, flexible repertoire for coping (Brent 1981). With such a broad repertoire, one has many different types of strategies to choose from; with a flexible repertoire, one can use them in different combinations. This style makes possible a wider range of responses to stress and thus the likelihood for more successfulchange and/or management.

Suggesting any one or more of the following strategies for coping will help students work toward both goals, because as coping behaviors are increased, stress is reduced. And students' stress is further reduced simply by the teacher's act of showing concern. The teacher's effect upon students should not be underestimated. To assist in making the impact as positive and helpful as possible, the following strategies are suggested for consideration.

Improve Study Habits
Many students describe their study habits as inadequate. It comes as no surprise then that they feel stressed. Being unprepared results in feeling out of control, which eventually increases stress (Bossing and Ruoff 1982). For those students, one solution toward higher levels of learning and lower levels of stress is a class in study skills. Most universities offer such a class, usually through the student counseling center. Research conducted in a variety of academic settings has demonstrated improved academic performance (Pauk 1974).

For students with reasonably good study habits but whose anxiety and fear of failure are interfering with their implementation, some specific study guides follow. These study guides, in combination with other techniques to reduce stress, will promote better preparation for class as well as a more positive cognitive appraisal for expectations of success (Pauk 1974).

- *Eliminate external distractions; find a good place to study.*
  - Dedicate that place to studying; don't use it for bull sessions, eating, and so on. It will then become a cue for study and will build the habit of studying when there.
  - Make sure the study area has good lighting, proper ventilation, a comfortable chair, and a table or desk large enough to spread out study materials. Gather all books, papers, pencils, and other tools *before* beginning.
  - Make sure the study place *does not* contain a stereo, television, telephone, refrigerator, or good view of the action.

- *Eliminate internal distractions.*
  Internal distractions are more difficult to eliminate
  than external ones. Reducing them is not a matter of
  will power but involves planning and finding ways to
  free the mind for studying.
  - Reduce indecision and daydreaming by deciding
    what to study when, by developing interest in class
    subjects, and by setting time limits for study.
  - If personal worries are distracting during study time,
    take positive steps to work on those problems. Set
    time aside to deal with them, either alone or with the
    help of friends or counselors.
  - Keep a card in the study area to write down appoint-
    ments and errands as they come to mind.
- *Eliminate physical and mental fatigue.*
  Physical health affects mental health; therefore, taking
  steps to improve one's health will also improve the
  ability to concentrate.
  - Eat a well-balanced diet that includes something
    from all major food groups each day and limit the
    consumption of caffeine. Caffeine is a stimulant that
    acts upon the body to arouse the central nervous
    system. People who ingest a lot of caffeine may not
    realize they are contributing to their stress, but caf-
    feine may interfere with sleep and the ability to con-
    centrate.
  - Get enough sleep—for most people seven to nine
    hours per night—and have a regular bedtime.
  - Find out what facilities and opportunities for exer-
    cise are available on campus and in the community
    and use them. Find one or two forms of enjoyable
    exercise that can fit into a student's schedule.
    Research indicates that health, endurance, and gen-
    eral well-being all depend on cardiovascular fitness,
    and the only way to achieve it is through regular
    exercise. Regular exercise is also a means of relaxa-
    tion and an adjunctive therapy in the treatment of
    depression and hypertension (Bowman and Allen
    1985).
  - Schedule study periods during the times of the day
    when you are most alert, divide study time among
    different subjects to reduce tedium, allot study
    breaks (10 minutes per hour) as a reward for good

concentration, and create interest in the subject being studied. Consider talking with a friend or acquaintance who is employed in a field related to the subject being studied. Find out more about its application in real life. Public television stations frequently cover a variety of topics and professional occupations that would enrich classroom learning. And consider a summer research project or work study program for even more exposure that will help in a future career.

Manage Time Wisely
Present time management to students as a way to work smarter, not harder, for one of the most important elements of working smarter is to practice time scheduling. Scheduling time gains most people more time (Lakein 1973) by doing a job in less time than it normally requires and by using leftover time that is normally wasted. To take advantage of leftover time, encourage students to record on paper their fixed activities so they can visualize potential blocks of time and begin to use them in a plan.

The following eight steps are suggested for maximum efficiency during study time.

- Plan your activities in a block of 50 minutes, followed by a 10-minute break.
- Use your most alert times of the day for studying.
- For a lecture-type class, use time immediately after class to review notes.
- For a recitation-type class (a foreign language, for example), use time immediately before the class to keep material fresh in your mind.
- Schedule your most important activities first to enable you to get them done on time. Start early.
- Allow eight hours of sleep a night and adequate time for eating a well-balanced meal.
- Start by allowing at least two hours of study for every hour of class time. Then adjust the schedule accordingly to master, not just cover, it.
- After trying your schedule, adjust it as necessary to create the best, and most workable, schedule for you. Some students do best with a detailed weekly schedule, others with a more simplified list of things to do.

The revision is the key to an effective schedule of living (Park 1974).

Learn Positive Self-Talk

Olympic athletes in one study exhibited some very different behavior, depending on whether they are "winners" or "losers" (Meichenbaum 1974). The winners had a very particular style of self-talk or inner dialogue that they used before and during the competitive event. This self-talk was distinguishable from the losers' self-talk in two important ways. First, the winners' talk was positive—"You're doing well," "You've worked hard and can win this event," "Good job!" Second, their talk was also relevant to the task—"First do this jump," "Get a good run for the bar." They became their own supportive coach, instructing themselves throughout the performance.

The losers, on the other hand, tended to engage in negative self-talk that was not relevant to the task—"What if I fall?" "I've got to win this event or I might as well quit." Their negative self-talk was more general than specific. It included more self-blame, catastrophizing, and anticipation of failure rather than success. Thus, because people tend to move in the direction of what they are thinking of most, those who think positively rather than negatively and focus on solutions rather than fears will direct themselves toward more successes in their lives (Waitley 1978).

Many of the concepts of self-talk and techniques developed from this research with athletes have also proven useful in academic settings (Goldfried, Linehan, and Smith 1978; Wine 1971). Psychologists and classes in learning skills now teach the importance of positive self-talk to students with test anxiety or any other stress-related problem interfering with learning or performance. First, students are asked to monitor their self-talk, especially before and during periods of anxiety, such as taking a test or making a presentation. Awareness of one's self-talk provides the baseline that will tell students more clearly what to do next. Those whose thoughts are self-defeating ("I'm going to fail this test and everyone's going to think I'm stupid") learn to replace them with more positive, task-relevant thoughts ("If I plan ahead and study well, chances are I won't fail. I'll do the best I can and use it as a first step in doing even better next time. Now, what is it I have to do?"). Positive and task-relevant self-talk appears to work because it promotes not only affective anticipations for success but also the behavioral acts (planning and studying) that are required for the actual outcome of success (for example, passing the test).

Learn How to Relax

What is relaxation and why does it lower stress? Relaxation is a physiological state that is incompatible with anxiety. Because the two states cannot coexist, when people are relaxed they cannot also be tense. Relaxation attacks predominantly physiological stress responses (pounding heart, rapid breathing, rising blood pressure) and facilitates the reduction of behavioral and cognitive stress responses.

The ability to relax in any situation serves two important purposes. First, keeping stress at a moderate level decreases daily wear and tear on the body. Second, it enables individuals to keep the self-control they need to decide how to handle stressful situations so as to decrease anxiety, anger, or fight-or-flight responses and thereby perform to their potential. Those able to stay calm, relaxed, and in control are more likely to be able to change stressful situations in positive ways. Those without this ability can be at the mercy of their stressors and react to them rather than act on them (Charlesworth and Nathan 1984).

Relaxation varies with each individual. Everyone has one or two ways to throw off the tensions that accumulate over the course of a day. When tension builds unrelieved over a long period of time, however, it becomes chronic stress; using a specific method of relaxation is an excellent technique for achieving noticeable results. When people learn to relax they do not lose motivation, slow down to the point of being less productive, or have to become a "laid-back" personality. In fact, people who do learn to relax tight muscles, eliminate pain from tension, and increase the intake of oxygen through deeper breathing report greater productivity, more energy, and less fatigue.

Those concerned that relaxation exercises consume too much time should be aware that after a week or so of practice, many forms of relaxation exercises can be cut to a few minutes. For example, training oneself to reach a relaxed state using progressive muscle relaxation involves a cue word or image associated with what relaxation feels like.

With practice, the goal is to be able to recall the feeling of being relaxed and in control by simply thinking of the cue word or image. This technique is especially useful when time or situations do not allow for the longer exercise.

A wide variety of relaxation methods are available. Most people find that one or two work best for them. The following list briefly describes several methods most commonly used and easily available. (More detail is available in *Life after Stress* (Shaffer 1982), *Controlling Stress and Tension* (Girdano and Everly 1986), and *Feeling Good* (Burns 1980).) Often a quick glance at chapter titles and exercises is helpful in deciding whether a reasonable match exists between an individual's needs and a book's content.

- *Breathing*. Breathing techniques are part of many effective forms of relaxation exercises. But they may also be of value in themselves. A regular, relaxed, slow pattern of breathing, achieved by moving the diaphragm rather than the upper chest, helps to lower arousal (shortness of breath, shaky voice), change physical indicators of a stress response (skin temperature), and supply more oxygen to the body, resulting in an overall feeling of well-being and control.
- *Progressive muscle relaxation*. Progressive relaxation can be learned using tapes or self-guidance. Both methods teach a process of tensing and relaxing muscle groups according to a particular sequence. With practice, people learn how to become deeply relaxed by scanning the body for tension and breathing deeply. The time it takes to become deeply relaxed grows briefer as skills are refined and cuing techniques mastered.
- *Meditation*. Several varieties of meditation exist, ranging from the very religious Eastern meditation to a more permissive and less mystical, clinically standardized meditation. Any type of meditation has certain essential elements, however: quiet surroundings, a passive attitude, a comfortable sitting position, and the *mantra*, a sound or phrase given to or chosen by the individual. During meditation, the individual repeats the mantra over and over as an aid in obliterating distracting thoughts and allowing feelings of restfulness, quiet, and a sense of well-being to develop.

Physiological effects like decreased heart rate, breathing rate, and blood pressure, and increased consumption of oxygen may occur.

- *Autogenic training.* Autogenic or self-generation techniques help control stress by training the autonomic nervous system to be more relaxed when no real need exists to fight or run. Autogenic training follows a natural progression *after* the individual has learned to control tension in the major muscle groups. It is accomplished by passively paying attention to verbal cues for relaxation—a sort of reprogramming the subconscious mind to create a state of internal calm.

- *Imagery.* Images are the mental pictures people create and "see" in their mind with eyes closed or open. Images can affect individuals strongly, and their influence can be positively or negatively arousing. Imagining sources of stimulation can create as great a physiologic response as the actual experience itself. For example, the image of squeezing lemon juice under the tongue increases salivation as effectively as doing so for many. Because of this phenomenon, many relaxation exercises use imagery alone or are coupled with muscle relaxation to achieve a deeply relaxed state. Some studies (Minsky 1978; Redmond et al. 1974) have further demonstrated the usefulness of imagery in the treatment of hypertension by suggesting that individuals visualize expanding arteries and their heart working slower and less forcefully. Another use of imagery for those who suffer performance or test anxiety or fear of failure is to visualize oneself successfully performing or passing a test while remaining relaxed and in control. Because people respond to their own perceptions of an event, training in keeping one's perceptions positive and manageable helps promote success (Lazarus 1977).

Join a Student Support Group

Most students can easily identify with the sentiment expressed by the following fourth-year medical student, who feels isolated and pressured to respond according to the expectations of others:

Burdened by the fabulous expectations of their parents and incessant scholastic demands, students must negoti-

ate a competitive course toward a goal they can scarcely envision. Their egos are routinely shattered by everyone from the secretaries at the admission office to the professor on rounds. It happens to practically everyone, but since their classmates are all pretending to be breezing through, there is little commiseration. Once home, they are expected to make up for their forced absence with lighthearted banter and passionate sex, even if they have been awake thirty-six hours watching a patient die. Their former friends accuse them of being rich doctors, when in fact their income qualifies them for food stamps. Through it all, they are reminded how lucky they are to have made it to medical school (Martin 1983, intro.).

Many of these situations happen to most students, but when "classmates are all pretending to be breezing through," little room is left for consolation or empathy.

Student support groups, however, represent a rejection of this unhealthy and competitive cycle by instead promoting openness and mutual support. In most universities, including law and medical schools, student support groups are considered one of the most useful and well-documented solutions to student stress (Finney 1975; Webster and Robinowitz 1979); nevertheless, they are rarely if ever included in the formal curriculum. Thus, their organization is left to students and faculty, typically two faculty members and a group of 8 to 12 students who together determine content, time, and duration. Content of the groups varies but usually reflects the interest, sophistication, and openness of its members.

- *Support groups* are built on group trust, and members learn to risk feelings (fear of failure, concerns about the future, interpersonal conflicts) in exchange for mutual support, problem solving, and the reassurance of knowing that they are not the only one struggling.
- *Career specialty groups* are comprised of community and academic professionals who describe their jobs, how they got them, their advantages and disadvantages. Students learn how their majors translate to real-world careers and lifestyles.
- *Literature groups* explore a career through the writings of a novelist or poet, providing an inroad to students' thoughts and feelings about a career.

- *Stress management groups* usually follow a plan of action and look for measurable improvement at the end.
- *Couples groups* present an opportunity for partners, especially spouses, to discuss school and career goals and share frustrations and dreams. They attempt to improve communication and problem-solving skills.

If students find that they are continuing to struggle with serious conflicts and anxiety that interfere with learning, faculty should encourage them to seek professional counseling or therapy. Faculty can increase a student's likelihood of following through with their recommendations by telling students exactly where the counseling services are located (virtually all institutions of higher learning provide counseling services for their students on campus), giving the student a specific phone number to call and if possible a counselor's name, learning how to explain the institution's fee-for-service system, reminding students that counseling sessions are strictly confidential, and being aware that the professor's own attitude toward counseling comes through loud and clear, strongly affecting a student's decision to obtain counseling.

A professor can also encourage students to live a healthy lifestyle. Proper nutrition, regular exercise, adequate sleep, and time spent with family and friends are essential for good physical health and mental alertness, both of them requirements for success in a long-term commitment like college. And the professor can ask students to become good observers of their own behavior. Adequate "self-information" is a prerequisite for students to become skilled at trusting their strengths and getting help in areas of weakness.

CONCLUDING RECOMMENDATIONS

The concept of stress inoculation as a guiding principle for reducing stress "involves giving people realistic warnings, recommendations, and reassurances to prepare them to cope with impending dangers and losses" (Janis 1982b, p. 259). Certainly feedback as well as the various suggestions discussed in this monograph for helping students help themselves are forms of warnings, recommendations, and reassurances. Even the recommendations about improving faculty-student relationships and the use of self-disclosure are forms of stress inoculation in that a positive relationship with faculty helps the student feel accepted as an individual of worth regardless of ability and background. Such information is valuable to students if stress is to be reduced and a sense of ambition and hope about their studies to increase (Ellinwood, Mayerson, and Paul 1983; Stevens 1973).

Interestingly enough, the primary concept associated with stress inoculation appears to be giving people information or educating them as to what is stressful, what to expect, and how best to cope. Yet research in higher education regarding professors' providing information to students in the classroom on how to deal with particular stresses of a course is not available. One thus does not know from the research how helpful it is in terms of reducing students' stress for professors to inform students about what to expect or how best to learn, or how best to recommend, reassure, or warn students about potential stressful aspects of a course.

The effects of information on reducing stress have been studied most extensively in the area of preparing soldiers for combat and in health-related fields (Janis 1982b). In fact, although the term "stress inoculation" was coined in 1977 (Meichenbaum 1977), the concept of battle inoculation was developed during World War II (Janis 1982b). Battle inoculation included informing soldiers with the use of films, pamphlets, and lectures about the realities of combat. Soldiers were also gradually exposed to actual combat but under reasonably safe conditions. The research suggests that the information and simulations of combat "served to reduce the disruptive effects of fear reaction in combat" (Janis 1982b, p. 12).

The results of studies on the effects of information in helping reduce stress among patients appear somewhat mixed, suggesting the possible complications of studying

The primary concept associated with stress inoculation appears to be giving people information or educating them as to what is stressful, what to expect, and how best to cope.

the concept of information in relation to students. Four basic types of information can be given to patients: information about the nature of a disease, medical procedures to be carried out, side effects to be expected, and strategies to cope with upcoming threats (Cohen and Lazarus 1979). Information has been found beneficial in several cases: reducing stress and enhancing recovery of cardiac patients (Rahe et al. 1975), reducing the need for pain medication in other patients (Langer, Janis, and Wolfer 1975) and in chronic pain patients (Turk and Genest 1979). The results of giving "accurate information about procedures or sensations to be expected [do] not show consistent effects in improving surgical outcomes," however (Cohen and Lazarus 1979, p. 249).

Some patients become even more anxious when efforts are made to prepare them psychologically with the use of information. Not every person benefits from all kinds of information about an illness; personality factors likely play an important role in determining who will benefit. Furthermore, it is difficult to know what kind of information presented in what way will benefit most people. Many confounding variables account for the mixed results of studies on information and stress reduction in patients. Certainly, similar factors will need to be considered in such studies of higher education. Such studies would be valuable, however, because the results would benefit teachers by giving them specific ideas about how information is helpful to which students and under what circumstances.

What, then, are areas for further research that would benefit professors in their attempts to help students overcome stress? One is the appropriate use of self-disclosure as well as other aspects of developing professional intimacy. It would be helpful to know what risk factors are associated with professional intimacy and self-disclosure and when, how, and under what circumstances they are most beneficial.

One aspect of developing professional intimacy involves the teacher as mentor. Research shows that mentors help reduce stress and increase learning when the relationship first develops but that eventually the relationship tends to deteriorate so that stress levels begin to increase. Further research could help determine why and how this change happens and—more important—how the deterioration can be avoided so that the benefits of having a mentor can be maintained, if not enhanced. The needs of both mentor and the student change over time; perhaps a quasi-experimental study could explore this relationship as it changes to compare successful and not so successful relationships.

Fairly limited research in education has shown the benefit of having students teach what they are studying (Benware and Deci 1984). Research to document the effects on learning of having students take more responsibility for teaching could be conducted. Under what circumstances is having a student teach most beneficial to his or her learning? That question is yet to be answered.

Although teachers can increase participation by asking questions of students, the technique often actually decreases participation when teachers do not wait more than one to two seconds before responding to their own questions (Rowe 1974). Research in this area has been conducted exclusively in elementary and high schools but not at the university level. Such research would be helpful to discover the optimal waiting time. It would also be helpful to know what kind of questioning elicits the best and most productive participation. It has been found, for example, that in law school the Socratic method of questioning is not necessarily useful for learning purposes and that in fact many students feel that it contributes to the high levels of stress they experience (Ellinwood, Mayerson, and Paul 1983; Stevens 1973), actually discouraging some students from participating.

One last area for further research involves stress among higher education faculty. The study by Gmelch, Lovrich, and Wilke (1984) is comprehensive but is only a first look at the sources of stress across many institutions. Further research needs to be conducted to see what input various institutional changes have on faculty members' stress levels, and experimentally designed studies to see how stress can be reduced would be helpful as well. Other studies should be conducted to observe how faculty stress affects students' stress and learning.

The research on stress in higher education—including its effects on learning and how best to work with it in the institution and the classroom—is still in its infancy. The third edition of the *Handbook of Research on Teaching* (Wittrock 1986), a project of the American Educational

Research Association, underscores this lack of research in that the word "stress" does not even appear in the subject index, test anxiety is barely mentioned in a few paragraphs, and only two sentences recognize the curvilinear relationship between anxiety and performance. The results of a recent nationwide survey (Astin 1986) that included nearly 200,000 freshman students who entered colleges or universities in 1985 seemd to justify the need for further research in the area of stress in higher education. Eight percent of the students surveyed said they feel depressed frequently, and 16 percent reported frequently feeling overwhelmed. Furthermore, approximately 50 percent of entering freshmen do not graduate from college, a decision associated with intense anxiety and stress and the combination of a long process of growing dissatisfaction (Hirsch and Keniston 1970). Further research might suggest the answers that would decrease that percentage.

REFERENCES

The ERIC Clearinghouse on Higher Education abstracts and indexes the current literature on higher education for the Office of Educational Research and Improvement's monthly bibliographic journal, *Resources in Education*. Most of these publications are available through the ERIC Document Reproduction Service (EDRS). For publications cited in this bibliography that are available from EDRS, ordering number and price are included. Readers who wish to order a publication should write to the ERIC Document Reproduction Service, 3900 Wheeler Avenue, Alexandria, Virginia 22304. When ordering, please specify the document number. Documents are available as noted in microfiche (MF) and paper copy (PC). Because prices are subject to change, it is advisable to check the latest issue of *Resources in Education* for current cost based on the number of pages in the publication.

Allen, Roger J. 1981. "Controlling Stress and Tension: Biomedical and Psychometric Evaluation of Programs at the University of Maryland." *Journal of School Health* 51 (5): 360–64.

American Psychiatric Association. 1980. *Diagnostic and Statistical Manual of Mental Disorders*. 3d ed. Washington, D.C.: APA.

Aspy, David, and Roebuck, Flora N. 1977. *Kids Don't Learn from People They Don't Like*. Amherst, Mass.: Human Resources Development Press.

Astin, Alexander W. 1986. *The American Freshman: National Norms for Fall 1985*. Los Angeles: American Council on Education and the University of California at Los Angeles.

Barnes-McConnell, Patricia W. 1980. "Leading Discussions." In *On College Teaching,* edited by Ohmer Milton. San Francisco: Jossey-Bass.

Barnett, David C., and Dalton, Jon C. November 1981. "Why College Students Cheat." *Journal of College Student Personnel* 22: 545–51.

Baum, Andrew; Singer, J. E.; and Baum, C. S. Winter 1981. "Stress and the Environment." *Journal of Social Issues* 37: 4–35.

Beck, Aaron T. 1967. *Depression: Clinical, Experimental, and Theoretical Aspects*. New York: Harper & Row.

Benware, Carl A., and Deci, Edward L. 1984. "Quality of Learning with an Active versus Passive Motivation Set." *American Educational Research Journal* 21: 755–65.

Biddle, Bruce J. 1964. "The Integration of Teacher Effectiveness Research." In *Contemporary Research on Teacher Effective-*

ness, edited by Bruce J. Biddle and William J. Ellena. New York: Holt, Rinehart & Winston.

Bossing, Lewis, and Ruoff, Nancy. 1982. "A Review of the Effects of Stress on the Teaching-Learning Process." Alexandria, Va.: ERIC Document Reproduction Service. ED 219 363. 42 pp. MF–$0.97; PC–$5.34.

Bouton, Clark, and Garth, Russell Y., eds. 1983. *Learning in Groups.* New Directions for Teaching and Learning No. 1H. San Francisco: Jossey-Bass.

Bowman, Marjorie A., and Allen, Deborah I. 1985. *Stress and Women Physicians.* New York: Springer-Verlag.

Boyer, Jenny L., and Guthrie, Lesley. 1985. "Assessment and Treatment of the Suicidal Patient." In *Handbook of Depression: Treatment, Assessment, and Research,* edited by E. E. Beckham and W. R. Leber. Homewood, Ill.: Dorsey Press.

Bradford, Leland P. 1958. "The Teaching-Learning Transaction." *Adult Education* 8 (3): 135–45.

Brent, David A. May 1981. "The Residency as a Developmental Process." *Journal of Medical Education* 56: 417–22.

Bruyn, H., and Seiden, R. 1965. "Student Suicide: Fact or Fancy?" *Journal of American College Health Association* 14 (1): 69–77.

Buck, Vernon E. 1972. *Working under Pressure.* New York: Crane, Russak & Co.

Burke, Ronald J. January/February 1971. "Are You Fed Up with Work?" *Personnel Administration* 34: 27–31.

Burns, David D. 1980. *Feeling Good: The New Mood Therapy.* New York: Signet.

Charlesworth, Edward A., and Nathan, Ronald G. 1984. *Stress Management.* New York: Ballantine Books.

Chickering, Arthur W. 1969. *Education and Identity.* San Francisco: Jossey-Bass.

Cohen, Frances, and Lazarus, Richard S. 1979. "Coping with the Stresses of Illness." In *Health Psychology,* edited by G. C. Stone, F. Cohen, and N. Adler. San Francisco: Jossey-Bass.

Cohen, Sheldon. July 1980. "Aftereffects of Stress on Human Performance and Social Behavior: A Review of Research and Theory." *Psychological Bulletin* 88: 82–108.

Comstock, Betsy S. 1984. "Suicide-Emergency Issues." In *Phenomenology and Treatment of Psychiatric Emergencies,* edited by B. S. Comstock et al. New York: Spectrum Publications.

Cooper, Cary L., and Marshall, Judi. March 1976. "Occupational Sources of Stress: A Review of the Literature Relating to Coronary Heart Disease and Mental Ill Health." *Journal of Occupational Psychology* 49: 11–28.

Davis, Keith E. February 1985. "Near and Dear: Friendship and Love Compared." *Psychology Today* 19: 22–30.

Davis, Robert H.; Fry, John P.; and Alexander, Lawrence. 1977. *The Discussion Method*. East Lansing: Michigan State University.

Dixon, Samuel L. 1979. *Working with People in Crisis: Theory and Practice*. St. Louis: C.V. Mosby.

Donald, Janet G. 1985. "The State of Research on University Teaching Effectiveness." In *Using Research to Improve Teaching*, edited by Janet G. Donald and Arthur M. Sullivan. New Directions for Teaching and Learning No. 23. San Francisco: Jossey-Bass.

Donald, Janet G., and Shore, Bruce M. 1977. "Student Learning and Evaluation of Teaching." In *If Teaching Is Important*, edited by Christopher K. Knapper et al. Waterloo, Ontario, Canada: Clarke, Irwin & Co.

Eble, Kenneth. 1979. *The Craft of Teaching*. San Francisco: Jossey-Bass.

Ellinwood, Steven; Mayerson, N.; and Paul, S. C. 1983. "Law Student Survey Results: An Empirical Method for Assessing Stress in Professional Education Programs: An Assessment of Stress among Law Students at the University of Utah." Mimeographed. Salt Lake City: University of Utah.

Ellner, Carolyn L., and Barnes, Carol P. 1983. *Studies of College Teaching: Experimental Results, Theoretical Interpretations, and New Perspectives*. Lexington, Mass.: Lexington Books, D.C. Heath.

Ericksen, Stanford C. 1984. *The Essence of Good Teaching*. San Francisco: Jossey-Bass.

Finney, Ben C. 1975. "The Peer Program: An Experiment in Humanistic Education." In *Psychological Stress in the Campus Community*, edited by B. Bloom. New York: Behavioral Publications.

Folkman, Susan. 1982. "An Approach to the Measurement of Coping." *Journal of Occupational Behavior* 3 (1): 95–107.

Gaff, Jerry G. 1973. "Making a Difference: The Impacts of Faculty." *Journal of Higher Education* 44 (8): 605–22.

Giannandrea, Vincenzo, and Murphy, Kevin C. November 1973. "Similarity Self-Disclosure and Return for a Second Interview." *Journal of Counseling Psychology* 20: 545–48.

Gibbard, G.; Hartman, J.; and Mann, R., eds. 1973. *Analysis of Groups: Contributions to Theory, Research, and Practice*. San Francisco: Jossey-Bass.

Girdano, Daniel A., and Everly, George S. 1986. *Controlling Stress and Tension: A Holistic Approach*. 2d ed. New York: Prentice-Hall.

Gmelch, Walter H.; Lovrich, Nicholas P.; and Wilke, Phyllis K. 1984. "Sources of Stress in Academe: A National Perspective." *Research in Higher Education* 20 (4): 477–90.

Goldfried, Marvin R.; Linehan, Marsha M.; and Smith, Jean L. 1978. "Reduction of Test Anxiety through Cognitive Restructuring." *Journal of Consulting and Clinical Psychology* 46 (1): 32–39.

Grites, Thomas J. 1980. "Improving Academic Advising." Idea Paper No. 3. Manhattan: Kansas State University, Center for Faculty Evaluation and Development in Higher Education.

Hansen, James C.; Stevic, Richard B.; and Warner, Richard W. 1977. *Counseling: Theory and Process*. Boston: Allyn & Bacon.

Hanson, Philip. 1975. "Giving Feedback: An Interpersonal Skill." *The 1975 Annual Handbook for Group Facilitators*. New York: University Associates Publishers.

Hechinger, Fred M. 28 October 1980 "Extraordinary Teachers Are Remembered." *The New York Times,*

Heins, Marilyn; Fahey, Shirley; and Leiden, Lisa. 1984. "Perceived Stress in Medical, Law, and Graduate Students." *Journal of Medical Education* 59 (3): 169–79.

Hildebrand, Milton. 1973. "The Character and Skills of the Effective Professor." *Journal of Higher Education* 44 (1): 41–50.

Hirsch, Steven J., and Keniston, Kenneth. February 1970. "Psychosocial Issues in Talented College Dropouts." *Psychiatry* 33: 1–20.

Hockey, Robert. 1979. "Stress and the Cognitive Components of Skilled Performance." In *Human Stress and Cognition,* edited by Vernon Hamilton and David M. Warbutin. New York: John Wiley & Sons.

Houston, B. Kent. March 1971. "Sources, Effects, and Individual Vulnerability of Psychological Problems for College Students." *Journal of Counseling Psychology* 18: 157–65.

Jacobson, Robert. 11 July 1984. "The Use of Humor by College Teachers Found to Stir Suspicion and Hostility." *Chronicle of Higher Education* 28: 25.

Janis, Irving L. 1982a. "Decision Making under Stress." In *Handbook of Stress: Theoretical and Clinical Aspects,* edited by L. Goldberger and Shlomo Bregnitz. New York: Free Press.

———. 1982b. *Stress, Attitudes, and Decisions: Selected Papers.* New York: Praeger.

Jourard, Sidney M. 1971. *The Transparent Self.* New York: Van Nostrand Co.

Kaplan, M. December 1980. "Patterns of Student Stress: A Profile of Teacher Education Students in Their First Year of Tertiary Studies." Report No. 13. Australia: Nedlands College of Advanced Education. ED 208 283. 63 pp. MF–$0.97; PC–7.14.

Katz, Joseph, et al. 1969. *No Time for Youth: Growth and Constraint in College Students.* San Francisco: Jossey-Bass.

Lakein, Alan. 1973. *How to Get Control of Your Time and Your Life.* New York: Signet.

Langer, Ellen J.; Janis, Irving L.; and Wolfer, John A. March 1975. "Reduction of Psychological Stress in Surgical Patients." *Journal of Experimental Social Psychology* 11: 155–65.

Lazarus, Arnold A. 1977. *In the Mind's Eye: The Power of Imagery for Personal Enrichment.* New York: Rawson Associates.

Lazarus, Richard S. 1966. *Psychological Stress and the Coping Process.* New York: McGraw-Hill.

Lazarus, Richard S., and Alfert, Elizabeth. August 1964. "The Short-Circuiting of Threat by Experimentally Altering Cognitive Appraisal." *Journal of Abnormal and Social Psychology* 69: 195–205.

Levinson, Daniel. 1978. *The Seasons of a Man's Life.* New York: Alfred A. Knopf.

Litman, Robert E., and Farberow, Norman L. 1961. *The Cry for Help.* New York: McGraw-Hill.

Lowman, Joseph. 1984. *Mastering the Techniques of Teaching.* San Francisco: Jossey-Bass.

Luepker, Russell V.; Johnson, C. Anderson; and Murray, David M. 1983. "Prevention of Cigarette Smoking: Three-Year Follow-Up of an Education Program for Youth." *Journal of Behavioral Medicine* 6 (1): 53–62.

Luria, Alexander R. 1932. *The Nature of Human Conflicts.* Translated by W. H. Gantt. New York: Liveright.

McCarter, W. Ronald. January 1974. "Making the Most of Subjectivity in Faculty Evaluation." *American Vocational Journal* 49: 32–33.

McCarthy, Patricia R., and Betz, Nancy E. July 1978. "Differential Effects of Self-disclosing versus Self-involving Counselor Statements." *Journal of Counseling Psychology* 25: 251–56.

Machlup, Fritz. October 1979. "Poor Learning from Good Teachers." *Academe:* 13: 376–80.

McKeachie, Wilbert J. 1979. "Student Ratings of Faculty: A Reprise." *Academe* 13: 384–97.

McLagan, Patricia. 1978. *Helping Others Learn.* Reading, Mass.: Addison-Wesley.

Mandler, George. 1982. "Stress and Thought Processes." In *Handbook of Stress: Theoretical and Clinical Aspects,* edited by L. Goldberger and Shlomo Bregnitz. New York: Free Press.

Mann, R. D. 1970. *The College Classroom: Conflict, Change, and Learning.* New York: John Wiley & Sons.

Mark, Sandra Fay. 1977. "Faculty Evaluation Systems: A Research Study of Selected Community Colleges in New York State." Photocopy. New York: Faculty Council of Community Colleges, State University of New York. ED 158 809. 152 pp. MF–$1.11; PC–$12.48.

Martin, B. 1975. "Parent-Child Relations." In *Review of Child Development Research,* vol. 4, edited by F. D. Horowitz. Chicago: University of Chicago Press.

Martin, Gary L., and Newman, Jan M. 1973. "The Costs and Effects of a Student Health Aide Program." *Journal of American College Health* 21 (6): 237–40.

Martin, Toni. 1983. *How to Survive in Medical School.* New York: Penguin Books.

Maslach, Christina. 1982. *Burnout—The Cost of Caring.* Englewood Cliffs, N.J.: Prentice-Hall.

Mechanic, David. 1978. *Students under Stress: A Study in the Social Psychology of Adaptation.* 2d rev. ed. Madison: University of Wisconsin Press.

Meeth, L. Richard. July 1976. "The Stateless Art of Teaching Evaluation." *Change Report on Teaching* 2: 3–5.

Meichenbaum, Donald. 1974. "The Clinical Potentials of Modifying What Clients Say to Themselves." In *Self-Control: Power to the Person,* edited by M. Mahoney and C. Thoreson. Monterey, Cal.: Brooks/Cole Publishing Co.

———. 1977. *Cognitive Behavior Modification: An Integrative Approach.* New York: Plenum Press.

———. 1985. *Stress Inoculation Training.* New York: Pergamon Press.

Menaghan, Elizabeth G. 1983. "Individual Coping Efforts: Moderators of the Relationship between Life Stress and Mental Health Outcomes." In *Psychosocial Stress: Trends in Theory and Research,* edited by H. B. Kaplan. New York: Academic Press.

Metalsky, Gerald I.; Abramson, Lyn Y.; Seligman, Martin E. P.; Semmel, Amy; and Peterson, Christopher. September 1982. "Attributional Style and Life Events in the Classroom: Vulnerability and Invulnerability to Depressive Mood Reactions." *Journal of Personality and Social Psychology* 43: 612–17.

Mikhail, Anis. 1985. "Stress: A Psychophysiological Conception." In *Stress and Coping,* edited by A. Monat and R. S. Lazarus. New York: Columbia University Press.

Minsky, P. J. 1978. "High Blood Pressure and Interpersonal Disengagement: A Study of Maladaptive Coping Styles and Ameliorative Treatments." Doctoral dissertation, Loyola University–Chicago.

Monk, G. Stephen. 1983. "Student Engagement and Student Power in Large Classes." In *Learning in Groups,* edited by Clark Bouton and Russell Y. Garth. New Directions for Teaching and Learning No. 1H. San Francisco: Jossey-Bass.

Mouw, David R. 1981. "Using the Personal (Very Personal) Anecdote." In *New Perspectives on Teaching and Learning.* New Directions for Teaching and Learning No. 7. San Francisco: Jossey-Bass.

Nedlands College of Advanced Education, Research Committee. 1980. *Patterns of Student Stress.* Report No. 13. Australia: Author. ED 208 283. 63 pp. MF–$0.97; PC–$7.14.

O'Hanlon, James, and Mortensen, Lynn. 1977. "Improving Teacher Evaluation." *CEDR Quarterly* 10 (6): 3–7.

Paine, Whiton S. 1982. *Job Stress and Burnout.* Beverly Hills, Cal.: Sage Publications.

Pascarella, Ernest T. 1980. "Student-Faculty Informed Contact and College Outcomes." *Review of Educational Research* 50: 545–95.

Pascarella, Ernest T.; Terezini, Patrick T.; and Hibel, James. 1978. "Student-Faculty Interactional Settings and Their Relationship to Predicted Academic Performance." *Journal of Higher Education* 49: 450–63.

Pauk, Walter. 1974. *How to Study in College.* 2d ed. New York: Houghton-Mifflin.

Peterson, Christopher, and Seligman, Martin E. P. 1985. "The Learned Helplessness Model of Depression: Current Status of Theory and Research." In *Handbook of Depression: Treatment, Assessment, and Research,* edited by E. E. Beckham and W. R. Leber. Homewood, Ill.: Dorsey Press.

Pines, Ayala M.; Aronson, Elliot; and Kafry, Ditsa. 1980. *Burnout.* New York: Free Press.

Rahe, Richard H.; O'Neil, Terry; Hagan, Arthur; and Arthur, Ranson J. 1975. "Brief Group Therapy Following Myocardial Infarction: Eighteen-Month Follow-up on Controlled Trial." *International Journal of Psychiatry in Medicine* 6 (3): 349–58.

Raimi, Ralph A. 26 April 1981. "Twice-Told Tale—The Joy of Teaching." *The New York Times Spring Survey of Education:* 59.

Redmond, D. P.; Gaylor, M. S.; McDonald, R. H.; and Shapiro, A. P. 1974. "Blood Pressure and Heart Rate Response to Verbal Instructions and Relaxation in Hypertension." *Psychosomatic Medicine* 36: 285–97.

Rizzolo, Patricia. 1982. "Peer Tutors Make Good Teachers." *Improving College and University Teaching* 30 (3): 115–19.

Robin, Sharon. 7 August 1985. "Professors, Students, and the Syllabus." *Chronicle of Higher Education* 30: 56.

Rogers, Carl R. 1969. *Freedom to Learn*. Columbus, Ohio: C. E. Merrill.

Rousseau, Denise M. 1976. "The Relationship of Task Characteristics to Attitudes, Absenteeism, Stress, and Performance among College Students." Alexandria, Va.: ERIC Document Reproduction Service. ED 140 181. 15 pp. MF–$0.97; PC–$5.34.

Rowe, Mary Budd. 1974. "Wait Time and Rewards as Instructional Variables, Their Influence on Language, Logic, and Fate Control. Part 1—Wait Time." *Journal of Research on Science Teaching* 11 (2): 81–94.

Sacco, William P., and Beck, Aaron T. 1985. "Cognitive Therapy of Depression." In *Handbook of Depression: Treatment, Assessment, and Research,* edited by E. E. Beckham and W. R. Leber. Homewood, Ill.: Dorsey Press.

Sadler, D. Royce. 1983. "Evaluation and the Improvement of Academic Learning." *Journal of Higher Education* 54 (1): 60–79.

Sarason, Irwin G. 1978. "The Test Anxiety Scale: Concept and Research." In *Stress and Anxiety,* vol. 5, edited by C. D. Spielberger and I. G. Sarason. New York: John Wiley & Sons.

Schwartz, William. 1980. "Education in the Classroom." *Journal of Higher Education* 51 (3): 235–54.

Scriven, Michael. 1967. *The Methodology of Evaluation*. AERA Monograph Series in Curriculum Evaluation No. 1. Chicago: Rand McNally.

———. 1981. "Summative Teacher Evaluation." In *Handbook of Teacher Evaluation,* edited by Jason Millman. Beverly Hills, Cal.: Sage Publications.

Seligman, Martin E. P. 1975. *Helplessness: On Depression, Development, and Death*. San Francisco: W. H. Freeman.

Selye, Hans. 1976. *The Stress of Life*. New York: McGraw-Hill.

Shaffer, Martin. 1982. *Life after Stress*. New York: Plenum Press.

Skinner, B. F. 1953. *Science and Human Behavior*. New York: Macmillan.

Spalt, Lee. 1980. "Suicide Behavior and Depression in University Student Psychiatric Referrals." *Psychiatric Quarterly* 52(4): 235–39.

Spielberger, Charles D.; Gonzalez, H. P.; Taylor, C. J.; Algaze, B.; and Anton, W. D. 1978. "Examination Stress and Test Anxiety." In *Stress and Anxiety: The Series in Clinical and Community Psychology,* edited by C. D. Spielberger and I. G. Sarason. New York: John Wiley & Sons.

Spitzer, Dean R. 1976. "The Instructional Developer as Behavioral Scientist." *NSPI Journal* 15 (4): 9–11.

Stevens, Robert. April 1973. "Law School and Law Students."
Virginia Law Review 59: 551–707.

Telch, Michael J.; Kellen, Joel D.; and McCoby, Nathan. 1982.
"Long-Term Follow-up of a Pilot Project on Smoking Prevention with Adolescents." *Journal of Behavioral Medicine* 5 (1):
1–8.

Terence, Tracey J., and Sherry, Patrick. September 1984. "College Student Distress as a Function of Person-Environment
Fit." *Journal of College Student Personnel* 25: 436–42.

Terezini, Patrick T.; Theophilides, Christos; and Lorang, Wen-
dell G. 1984. "Influences on Students' Perceptions of Their
Academic Skill Development during College." *Journal of
Higher Education* 55: 621–36.

Torbert, William R. 1978. "Educating toward Shared Purpose,
Self-direction, and Quality Work." *Journal of Higher Education* 49: 109–35.

Turk, Dennis C., and Genest, Myles. 1979. "Regulation of Pain:
The Application of Cognitive and Behavioral Techniques for
Prevention and Remediation." In *Cognitive-Behavioral Inter-
ventions: Theory, Research, and Practice,* edited by P. Kendall
and S. Hollard. New York: Academic Press.

Waitley, Dennis. 1978. *Psychology of Winning.* Chicago:
Nightingale-Conant.

Webster, Thomas G., and Robinowitz, Carol B. January 1979.
"Becoming a Physician: Long-Term Student Group." *General
Hospital Psychiatry* 1: 53–61.

Whitman, Neal, and Schwenk, Thomas L. 1983. *A Handbook for
Group Discussion Leaders: Alternatives to Lecturing Medical
Students to Death.* Salt Lake City: University of Utah School
of Medicine. ED 233 623. 38pp. MF–$0.97; PC not available
EDRS.

———. 1984. *Preceptors as Teachers: A Guide to Clinical Teaching.* Salt Lake City: University of Utah School of Medicine.
ED 266 727. 30pp. MF–$0.97; PC not available EDRS.

Whitman, Neal; Spendlove, David; and Clark, Claire. 1984. *Student Stress: Effects and Solutions.* ASHE-ERIC Higher Education Report No. 2. Washington, D.C.: Association for the
Study of Higher Education. ED 246 832. 115 pp. MF–$0.97;
PC–$10.74.

Whitman, Neal, and Weiss, Elaine. 1982. *Faculty Evaluation:
The Use of Explicit Criteria for Promotion, Retention, and
Tenure.* AAHE-ERIC Higher Education Research Report No.
2. Washington, D.C.: American Association for Higher Education. ED 221 148. 57 pp. MF–$0.97; PC–$7.14.

Wine, J. 1971. "Test Anxiety and Direction of Attention." *Psychological Bulletin* 76 (2): 92–104.

Wittrock, Merlin C., ed. 1986. *Handbook of Research on Teaching.* 3d ed. New York: Macmillan.

Yerkes, Robert M., and Dodson, J.D. November 1908. "The Relation of Strength of Stimulus to Rapidity of Habit Formation." *Journal of Comparative and Neurological Psychology* 18: 459–82.

INDEX

A

Academic advising, 36
Academic community: sense of, 36, 38–39
Academic performance: influences on, 35–36
Academic status: establishment of, 17–19
Accessibility of faculty, 27, 35–36
Achievement need, 3, 4
Active listening, 45
Alcohol, 46
Alcott, A. Bronson, 35
American Educational Research Association, 65–66
Analytic/synthetic teaching approach, 6–7
Anecdotes: use of, 34
Anger, 10, 51, 58
Anxiety, 10, 41, 44, 51, 58, 66
Anxious-dependent students, 41–42
Assignments
    justification, 25
    technique for learning names, 32
    weekly, 19
    written/positive comments, 42
Athletes: self-talk, 57
Attention narrowing, 13, 14
Authoritarian teaching style, 9
Avoidance, 12, 13

B

"Battle inoculation," 63
Behavioral reactions to test-taking, 13
Berg, Paul, 29
Biofeedback, 52
Biological stressors, 10
Boredom, 10, 41
Buddy systems, 52
Burnout, 51–52

C

Career specialty groups, 61
Challenges, 4
Cheating, 18
Clark, Kenneth, 29
Class participation, 31–32
Class size, 18, 22
Cognitive fatigue, 14
Cognitive reappraisal, 52
Conceptual understanding, 33

Faculty
> accessibility, 27, 35–36
> advising skills, 36–37
> burnout, 51–52
> course goals, 5
> influential, 29
> interaction with students, 15, 29–39
> job satisfaction, 50
> meetings with students, 22–23, 44–45
> mentor role, 37–38
> nonverbal communication, 45
> "professional intimacy," 34–35
> rapport with students, 7, 33–34, 49
> research, 38
> role in learning, 1–5
> role in stress reduction, 14, 47, 62, 63
> role models, 35, 38
> self-disclosure/self-awareness, 48–52
> stress, 15, 65
> workload, 51

Failure, 12, 42, 43
Family influence, 15
Fatigue, 10, 14, 55, 58
Fear, 10, 41, 44, 58
Fear of failure, 3, 4, 60
Feedback
> establishing academic status, 17–19
> learning loops, 19–20
> personal meetings, 22–23
> solicitation from students, 26–28
> stress reducer, 15, 63
> written comments, 20–22

Food indulgence, 46
Freshmen
> orientation, 1
> self-direction, 30
> stress level, 66

G

General Adaption Syndrome, 10
Global thinking patterns, 42–43
Goal-directed behavior, 3
Goals: courses, 5, 6
"Good stress," 53
Grades vs. written comments, 20
Group discussion, 31

Guidelines
  classroom humor, 34
  facilitator, 2
Guilt, 44

H
Health, 55, 62
Helplessness, 41
Humor in the classroom, 33–34
Hypervigilance, 13, 14

I
Imagery: relaxation technique, 60
Incentives, 4
Index cards as feedback mechanism, 27
Information as stress reducer, 15
Inoculation against destructive stress, 15
Instruction (see Teaching)
Instructor/group interaction, 7
Interpersonal skills, 52
Introductory courses: test types, 25

L
Laissez-faire teaching style, 9
Large classes, 22
Law schools, 61, 65
Learning
  as measure of teaching, 5
  need for structure, 30
  relationship to teaching, 1–8
Learning loops, 19–20
Lifestyle, 62
Listening skills, 37, 45
Literature groups, 61
Logs: as structure mechanism, 30
Loss, 12
Luria, Alexander, 13

M
Medical school, 11, 60–61
Meditation, 59–60
Meetings
  as feedback, 22–23
  reactions to stress, 44–45
Memorization, 17, 18, 25, 33
Mentors, 37–38, 64
Military stress reduction, 63
Motivation, 1, 2–4, 28

Timing of feedback, 21
Tutors: use of, 32–33, 42

U

Unconflicted change, 12
Unconflicted inertia, 12
University of Maryland: stress management course, 52
University of New Mexico: humor study, 33
University of Utah
    law student stress study, 15
    learning loops: retaking tests, 19

V

Vigilance in decision-making, 12

W

Weekly assignments, 19
Women and mentors, 37–38
Work environment, 50–51
Workload, 51
Worry reduction, 14
Worthlessness, 44
Written comments as learning loop, 20

Y

Yerkes-Dodson law, 9

ASHE-ERIC HIGHER EDUCATION REPORTS

Starting in 1983, the Association for the Study of Higher Education
assumed cosponsorship of the Higher Education Reports with the ERIC
Clearinghouse on Higher Education. For the previous 11 years, ERIC and
the American Association for Higher Education prepared and published
the reports.

Each report is the definitive analysis of a tough higher education problem, based on a thorough research of pertinent literature and institutional
experiences. Report topics, identified by a national survey, are written by
noted practitioners and scholars with prepublication manuscript reviews
by experts.

Eight monographs (10 monographs before 1985) in the ASHE-ERIC
Higher Education Report series are published each year, available indi-
vidually or by subscription. Subscription to eight issues is $60 regular; $50
for members of AERA, AAHE, and AIR; $40 for members of ASHE.
(Add $7.50 outside the United States.)

Prices for single copies, including 4th class postage and handling, are
$10.00 regular and $7.50 for members of AERA, AAHE, AIR, and ASHE
($7.50 regular and $6.00 for members for 1983 and 1984 reports, $6.50
regular and $5.00 for members for reports published before 1983). If faster
1st class postage is desired for U.S. and Canadian orders, add $.75 for
each publication ordered; overseas, add $4.50. For VISA and MasterCard
payments, include card number, expiration date, and signature. Orders
under $25 must be prepaid. Bulk discounts are available on orders of 15 or
more reports (not applicable to subscriptions). Order from the Publications Department, Association for the Study of Higher Education, One
Dupont Circle, Suite 630, Washington, D.C. 20036, 202/296-2597. Write
for a publication list of all the Higher Education Reports available.

1986 Higher Education Reports

1. Post-tenure Faculty Evaluation: Threat or Opportunity?
   Christine M. Licata

2. Blue Ribbon Commissions and Higher Education: Changing Academe
   from the Outside
   Janet R. Johnson and Laurence R. Marcus

3. Responsive Professional Education: Balancing Outcomes and
   Opportunities
   Joan S. Stark, Malcolm A. Lowther, and Bonnie M.K. Hagerty

4. Increasing Students' Learning: A Faculty Guide to Reducing Stress
   among Students
   Neal A. Whitman, David C. Spendlove, and Claire H. Clark

1985 Higher Education Reports

1. Flexibility in Academic Staffing: Effective Policies and Practices
   Kenneth P. Mortimer, Marque Bagshaw, and Andrew T. Masland

2. Associations in Action: The Washington, D.C., Higher
   Education Community
   Harland G. Bloland

3. And on the Seventh Day: Faculty Consulting and Supplemental
   Income
   Carol M. Boyer and Darrell R. Lewis

Increasing Students' Learning

4. Faculty Research Performance: Lessons from the Sciences and Social Sciences
   John W. Creswell

5. Academic Program Reviews: Institutional Approaches, Expectations, and Controversies
   Clifton F. Conrad and Richard F. Wilson

6. Students in Urban Settings: Achieving the Baccalaureate Degree
   Richard C. Richardson, Jr., and Louis W. Bender

7. Serving More Than Students: A Critical Need for College Student Personnel Services
   Peter H. Garland

8. Faculty Participation in Decision Making: Necessity or Luxury?
   Carol E. Floyd

1984 Higher Education Reports

1. Adult Learning: State Policies and Institutional Practices
   K. Patricia Cross and Anne-Marie McCartan

2. Student Stress: Effects and Solutions
   Neal A. Whitman, David C. Spendlove, and Claire H. Clark

3. Part-time Faculty: Higher Education at a Crossroads
   Judith M. Gappa

4. Sex Discrimination Law in Higher Education: The Lessons of the Past Decade
   J. Ralph Lindgren, Patti T. Ota, Perry A. Zirkel, and Nan Van Gieson

5. Faculty Freedoms and Institutional Accountability: Interactions and Conflicts
   Steven G. Olswang and Barbara A. Lee

6. The High-Technology Connection: Academic/Industrial Cooperation for Economic Growth
   Lynn G. Johnson

7. Employee Educational Programs: Implications for Industry and Higher Education
   Suzanne W. Morse

8. Academic Libraries: The Changing Knowledge Centers of Colleges and Universities
   Barbara B. Moran

9. Futures Research and the Strategic Planning Process: Implications for Higher Education
   James L. Morrison, William L. Renfro, and Wayne I. Boucher

10. Faculty Workload: Research, Theory, and Interpretation
    Harold E. Yuker

1983 Higher Education Reports

1. The Path to Excellence: Quality Assurance in Higher Education
   Laurence R. Marcus, Anita O. Leone, and Edward D. Goldberg

NOTES

Quantity		Amount

Please enter my subscription to the 1986 ASHE-ERIC Higher Education Reports at $60.00, 25% off the cover price. _____

Please enter my subscription to the 1987 Higher Education Reports at $60.00 _____

I certify that I am a member of AAHE, AERA, or AIR (circle one) and qualify for the special rate of $50.00.

_____ 1986 series subscription _____
_____ 1987 series subscription _____

I certify that I am a member of ASHE and qualify for the special rate of $40.00.

_____ 1986 series subscription _____
_____ 1987 series subscription _____

Individual reports are available at the following prices:
1985 and forward, $10.00 each ($7.50 for members).
1983 and 1984, $7.50 each ($6.00 for members).
1982 and back, $6.50 each ($5.00 for members).

Please send me the following reports:

(Title)

_____ Report No. _____ (_____) _____
_____ Report No. _____ (_____) _____
_____ Report No. _____ (_____) _____

SUBTOTAL: _____
Optional 1st Class Shipping ($.75 per book) _____
TOTAL AMOUNT DUE: _____

NOTE: All prices subject to change.

Name _____

Title _____

Inst. _____

Addr. _____

City _____ ST _____ Zip _____

Phone _____

Signature _____

☐ Check enclosed, payable to ASHE.
☐ Please charge my credit card:
    ☐ Visa ☐ MasterCard (check one)

Expiration date _____

ASHE ERIC®

Association for the Study of Higher Education
The George Washington University
One Dupont Circle, Suite 630, Dept. E
Washington, D.C. 20036
Phone: (202) 296-2597

Did you remember:
1. To enclose your method of payment?
2. To indicate clearly which reports you wanted?
3. To sign and date your check?
4. To put postage on this card?

Thank you for your order. Please allow 3–4 weeks for delivery.

Please fold along dotted line and staple close

FROM: _____

_____

_____

_____

Place
Stamp
Here

Association for the Study of Higher Education
One Dupont Circle, Suite 630, Dept. E
Washington, DC 20036